The Encyclopedia of
North American Indians

Volume IX

Ross, John – Trail of Broken Treaties

General Editor
D. L. Birchfield

Marshall Cavendish

Published in 1997 by
Marshall Cavendish Corporation
99 White Plains Road
Tarrytown, NY 10591-9001
U.S.A.

Developed, designed, and produced by Water Buffalo Books, Milwaukee

Project director: Mark J. Sachner
General editor: D. L. Birchfield
Art director: Sabine Beaupré
Photo researcher: Diane Laska
Project editor: Valerie J. Weber

Editors: Elizabeth Kaplan, MaryLee Knowlton, Judith Plumb, Carolyn Kott Washburne

Consulting editors: Donna Beckstrom, Jack D. Forbes, Annette Reed Crum, John Bierhorst

Picture credits: © B. & C. Alexander: 1201, 1202, 1287, 1290, 1291; © Archive Photos: 1162, 1172, 1176, 1198, 1238; © Archive Photos/AFP: 1225; © Steve Bly: 1191, 1192; © Kit Breen: 1200, 1250, 1263, 1280; © Brown Brothers, Sterling, PA: 1237, 1251, 1269, 1278; Courtesy of Joseph Bruchac: 1241; © Corbis-Bettmann: 1161, 1167, 1183, 1186, 1190, 1206, 1212, 1224, 1230, 1245, 1253, 1267, 1271, 1282, 1283, 1294; © Culver Pictures: 1163; Photo © Addison Doty, Courtesy of Morning Star Gallery: 1159; © Barry Durand, Odyssey Productions: 1184; © Steven Ferry: 1177, 1178; © Robert Frerck, Odyssey Productions: 1208, 1215, 1232, 1234, 1293; © Hampton University Archives, Hampton, Virginia: 1193; © 1982 Corson Hirschfeld: 1181; © 1993 Millie Knapp: 1187; © 1995 Millie Knapp: 1166; © 1996 Millie Knapp: 1228; © Brad Markel/Gamma Liaison: 1209; Collection of Moshe ben-Shimon: 1179; © Odyssey Productions: 1204, 1205, 1259; The Philbrook Museum of Art, Tulsa, Oklahoma: Cover; © Antonio Ribeiro/Gamma Liaison: 1182; © Renato Rotolo/Gamma Liaison: 1221, 1268; © STOCK MONTAGE, INC.: 1157, 1207, 1252, 1274; © Stephen Trimble: title, 1160, 1165, 1168, 1169, 1188, 1189, 1199, 1222, 1223, 1231, 1248, 1249, 1260, 1261, 1262, 1275, 1276, 1277, 1281, 1288, 1289; © UPI/Corbis-Bettmann: 1171, 1174 (both), 1194, 1196, 1218, 1266, 1285, 1296

Library of Congress Cataloging-in-Publication Data

The encyclopedia of North American Indians.
　　　　p.　cm.
　　　Includes bibliographical references and index.
　　　Summary: A comprehensive reference work on the culture and history of Native Americans.
　　　ISBN 0-7614-0236-5 (vol. 9)　　ISBN 0-7614-0227-6 (lib. bdg.: set)
　　　1. Indians of North America--Encyclopedias, Juvenile.
　　[1. Indians of North America--Encyclopedias.]
　　E76.2.E53　1997
　　970.004'97'003--dc20　　　　　　　　　　　　　　96-7700
　　　　　　　　　　　　　　　　　　　　　　　　　　　CIP
　　　　　　　　　　　　　　　　　　　　　　　　　　　AC

Printed and bound in Italy

Title page illustration: A mural at the Santa Fe Indian School in New Mexico depicts the balanced relationship among various life forces in our world.

Editor's note: Many systems of dating have been used by different cultures throughout history. *The Encyclopedia of North American Indians* uses B.C.E. (Before Common Era) and C.E. (Common Era) instead of B.C. (Before Christ) and A.D. (Anno Domini, "In the Year of the Lord") out of respect for the diversity of the world's peoples.

Contents

ROSS, JOHN (1790–1866)

John Ross (Coowescoowe or "The Egret") was born along the Coosa River at Tahnoovayah, Georgia (near Lookout Mountain). The third of nine children, he would become the founder of a Cherokee constitutional government. His father was Daniel Ross, a Scot, and his mother, Mary (Molly) McDonald, was a Scot-Cherokee woman. As a youth, he was called Tsan-usdi or "Little John."

Although brought up with other Cherokees, Ross was educated at home by non-Indian tutors and then continued his education at Kingston Academy in Tennessee. Although he was only about one-eighth Cherokee, Ross always identified himself as Cherokee and was married in 1813 to "Quatie" or Elizabeth Brown Henley, a full-blooded Cherokee. They had five children.

Ross began his political career in 1809 when he went on a mission to the Arkansas Cherokees. By 1811, he was serving as a member of the standing committee of the Cherokee Council. In 1813–1814, he was an adjutant in a Cherokee regiment under the command of General Andrew Jackson and saw action with other Cherokees at Horseshoe Bend in 1813 against the Red Sticks commanded by "Red Eagle" (William Weatherford). Ross led a contingent of Cherokee warriors in a diversionary tactic and thus was an important factor in Jackson's success at Horseshoe Bend.

In 1814, shortly after his marriage, Ross set up a ferry service and trading post at Ross's Landing. In 1817, he became a member of the Cherokee National Council; he served as president of the National Council from 1819 to 1826. In 1820, the Cherokee people instituted a republican form of government, similar in structure to that of the United States. As an advocate of education and mission work among his people, Ross thought that the Cherokees might become a state in the union, with its own constitution. When New Echota, Georgia, became the Cherokee national capital in 1826, Ross moved there with his family. In 1827, he

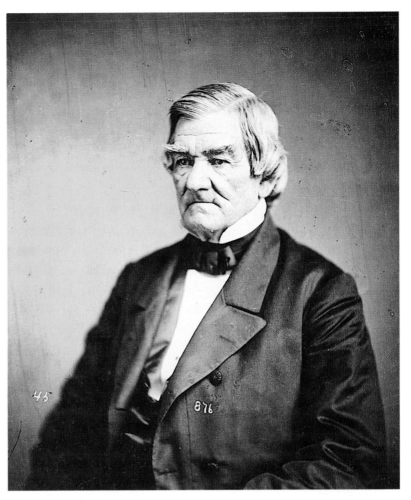

Although John Ross was only one-eighth Cherokee, he identified himself as a Cherokee and distinguished himself in the Cherokee political realm. He used his diplomatic skills in his dealings with fellow Cherokees, other Indian groups, and the United States government.

became president of the Cherokee constitutional convention, which drafted a new constitution. From 1828 to 1839, Ross served as principal chief of the Cherokee Nation under this new constitution.

During Ross's years as chief, he opposed federal and state encroachments on tribal lands. He resisted Georgia's contention that the Cherokees were mere tenants on state lands. When Georgia stripped the Cherokees of their civil rights between 1828 and 1831, Ross took their case to the Supreme Court and won, but President Andrew Jackson violated his oath of office by defying the Supreme Court when he refused to enforce the decision. With the discovery of gold near Dahlonega, Georgia, non-Native officials pressed for the relocation westward of the Cherokees along with other eastern American Indians. Jackson also signed the Indian Removal Act of 1830, which provided for the relocation of eastern tribes west of the Mississippi in an area that would become Indian Territory (today's Oklahoma).

Although Ross continued to resist removal policies as principal chief of the Cherokees, a dispirited minority of Cherokee leaders called the Treaty Party, including John Ridge, Major Ridge, Elias Boudinot, and Stand Watie, consented to removal by signing the Treaty of New Echota in 1835. Ross and a majority of the Cherokees sought to have the treaty withdrawn and sent a letter to Congress in 1836 asking for an investigation into its legality.

Although Ross continued to protest removal for three more years, the state of Georgia started to coerce the Cherokees into selling their lands for a fraction of their real value. Marauding European-Americans plundered Cherokee homes and possessions and destroyed the *Cherokee Phoenix's* printing press because it opposed removal. The U.S. Army forced Cherokee families into internment camps to prepare for the arduous trek westward. As a result of unhealthy and crowded conditions in these hastily constructed stockades, many Cherokees died even before the trek, known as the Trail of Tears, began. While failing in his efforts to stop removal, Ross managed to gain additional federal funds for his people.

During the internment of the Cherokees in Georgia and the two disastrous trips along the Trail of Tears, over four thousand Cherokees died of exposure, disease, and starvation—about one-quarter of the total Cherokee population. Quatie, Ross's wife, was among the victims of this forced emigration. After removal, the miserable conditions did not cease; many Cherokees died after they arrived in Indian Territory as epidemics and food shortages plagued the new settlements.

Upon his arrival in Indian Territory, Ross joined the Western Cherokees who had moved several years earlier. He aided in the drafting of the constitution for the United Cherokees and served as its head from 1839 until his death in 1866. In 1839, with the assassination of the Ridges and Boudinot in retaliation for their role in signing the removal treaty, tribal factions became polarized and some of the proponents of the Treaty Party claimed that Ross had a role in the assassinations, but they never produced any evidence. Sequoyah, the originator of the Cherokee alphabet, and other peacemakers sought to reconcile the factions within the tribe. In 1844, Ross remarried a Quaker woman named Mary Bryan Stapler, and they had three children. Between 1839 and 1856, he went to Washington five times seeking justice for his people.

Although Ross was a large slaveholder when the U.S. Civil War began, he opposed a Cherokee alliance with the Confederacy. Instead, he advocated Cherokee neutrality. Many of Ross's supporters were opposed to slavery. By the summer of 1861, many influential leaders, including Stand Watie, favored joining the Confederacy. Ross convened a national conference and was overruled by the pro-Confederacy forces. By 1862, federal troops had regained control over most of Indian Territory, so Ross moved his wife and family to Kansas. The Southern Cherokees under Stand Watie formed a separate government that still allied with the Confederacy. Faced with such tragic divisions, Ross went to Washington to tell President Abraham Lincoln about the rebellious Southern Cherokees.

At the end of the Civil War, the Cherokees were deeply split. Ross, at seventy-five and in bad health, journeyed to Washington as the head of the Northern Cherokees for new treaty negotiations that sought to protect the Cherokees and their constitution. He died while in Washington on August 1, 1866, during negotiations. His body was returned to Indian Territory and was buried at Park Hill, Oklahoma.

— B. E. Johansen

SEE ALSO:

Boudinot, Elias; Cherokee; Cherokee Alphabet; *Cherokee Phoenix*; Jackson, Andrew; Oklahoma; Removal Act, Indian; Sequoyah; Trail of Tears; Watie, Stand.

RUG, NAVAJO

Navajos say that they have always known how to weave, that it was taught to them by Spider Woman, the deity who wove together lightning, rainbows, clouds, and sunbeams on a giant loom to form the universe and by her example taught people on earth how to weave. The earliest evidence of Navajo weaving is in the form of yucca fronds woven into large mats, used to cover a light frame of poles. The poles and mats formed the roof for a mobile shelter, a covering for a shallow pit. When camp was moved, the light poles and mats were carried to the new location.

Despite this evidence of early Navajo weaving, ethnologists say that there can be little doubt that Navajos learned the art of the loom and the weaving of rugs from the Pueblos. Close contact with the Pueblos during the Spanish colonial era is known to have had a far-reaching cultural influence on the Navajos, and the use of the loom is thought to have been one of the by-products of the intimate contact between the two cultures during that era. Ethnologists point out that there has never been any evidence of Navajo loomed products in any material other than wool, and that the Navajos are known to have acquired sheep from the Spanish and the Pueblos. The use of the loom is thought to have spread to the Navajos through intermarriage with Pueblos.

Loom weaving is an art that cannot be learned by casual observation. It requires many years of careful instruction. Among the Navajos it is an art practiced by the women, but among the Pueblos it is an art practiced by the men. It has been suggested that Pueblo weavers who intermarried among the Navajos were unable to interest their sons in the art, because Navajo culture provided a different role for the men, and so the weavers taught the art to their daughters. Regardless of how the art form came to be a part of Navajo culture, it soon became an important cultural and economic activity, and Navajos quickly became internationally famous for their weaving.

Navajo weaving has undergone many changes in designs. Navajos are continually creating new ones, and various locations within the Navajo

This Navajo rug, which is made out of homespun yarns and a commercially manufactured dye, was woven sometime between 1900 and 1915.

Nation have become famous for particular types of rugs and patterns. Materials woven between 1850 and 1875 are said to be from the Classic period of Navajo weaving. A transitional period followed, from 1875 to 1890, during which the Navajos adapted their methods and designs to satisfy the demands of the tourist trade. Men who operated trading

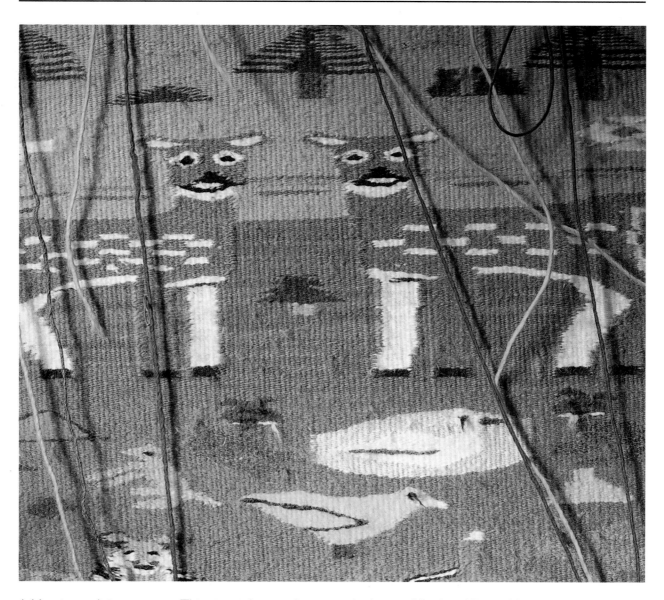

A Navajo work in progress. This pictorial rug is shown on the loom of Pauline Allen, a Navajo weaver in Tsaile, Arizona.

posts within the Navajo Nation, such as Lorenzo Hubbell, encouraged Navajo women to begin weaving larger blankets that could be used as rugs, which required hundreds of hours to make. The traders then produced colorful catalogs displaying the creativity of the weavers and sent them to merchants in the East. Railroads helped provide a means of getting the rugs to distant markets, and Navajo rugs soon became widely known. Twentieth-century innovations have included the use of commercial dyes to produce brighter colors.

Weaving underwent a revival in the 1920s, when Chinle weavers introduced the multicolored Wide Ruins, Crystal, and Pine Springs patterns. The rug weavers' auction at Crownpoint, in the Navajo Checkerboard portion of northwestern New Mexico, is internationally known. Sometimes the rugs bring a good price. In 1987, a Two Grey Hills weaving, a 5-x-8 1/2-foot (153-x-260-centimeter) tapestry woven by Barbara Ornelas and her sister Rosann Teller Lee, won Best of Show at the Santa Fe Indian Market and sold for sixty thousand dollars. The sisters had worked on the tapestry for four years. Weaving remains an important economic activity throughout the Navajo Nation, one which is pursued with great pride and which is handed down from generation to generation.

SEE ALSO:

Navajo; Navajo Reservation; Pueblo; Spider Woman.

SAC AND FOX

The Sac and the Fox are two separate, independent Indian nations, although they are both of the Algonquian language family and have been closely allied and affiliated since they settled in Indian Territory (present-day Oklahoma) in the 1860s. Since then, they have been classified as one nation and are referred to as the Sac and Fox.

Historically, the Sac have been known as the Sauk, which means "people of the outlet" or "people of the yellow earth." The Fox people's real name is Meshkwakihug (or, more commonly, Mesquakie), which means "red earth people." Early French settlers called the people Fox based on the name Red Fox, which was one of the clan names of the tribe.

The Sac and Fox were of the Eastern Woodlands (roughly, the northeastern quadrant of the United States and parts of southeastern Canada), and they lived in the Great Lakes region. They used shells for utensils and were skilled in making canoes. They lived in fixed villages but made long buffalo hunting expeditions.

Early in the 1700s, the Sac and the Fox peoples were pushed southward, out of the Great Lakes region, by the French and the Ojibwes (Chippewas). At this time, though they formed a strong alliance, they each kept their separate tribal identities. Some of them settled in northwestern Illinois, while another group settled west of the Mississippi River.

Like other Native groups both before and throughout the European settlement of the Americas, the Sac and the Fox formed various alliances with—and engaged in an assortment of hostilities against—other Indian tribes. Often, these alliances were in concert with the actions of whites and were designed to serve the best interests of the respective tribes. When white settlers made war against the Indians in the Illinois area, the Sac and Fox were allied with bands of Potawatomi and the Kickapoo. They were later allied with the British in the American Revolution and from 1811 through 1813 were a part of Tecumseh's Confederacy, the goal of which was to stop U.S. expansion west of the Ohio River Valley. This alliance again put them

This 1833–1834 illustration by Karl Bodmer depicts two members of what would come to be known as the Sac and Fox. On the left is a member of the Sac (Sauk) tribe, on the right a member of the Fox.

This photographic portrait, taken in the 1890s, is of a member of the Sac and Fox in Oklahoma Territory, just a few years before what was once called Indian Territory became the state of Oklahoma.

on the side of the British, this time in the War of 1812.

The Sac and Fox of Missouri, the band that had settled west of the Mississippi, signed a treaty that led to the cession of their lands on both sides of the Mississippi to the United States. This treaty, known as the Treaty of 1804, caused much friction between the two bands.

From 1831 through 1832, the Sauk leader Black Hawk rallied his people's Native allies to stand up for their rights and remain in Illinois when settlers and government officials seized the Fox lead mines west of the Mississippi. His forces were defeated in what became known as Black Hawk's War, and he was imprisoned for his role in leading the rebellion. He was later paroled and died in Iowa in 1838.

After Black Hawk's War, the Sac and the Fox moved west into Iowa and forced the Sioux out of that country. Through a series of treaties, all Sac and Fox lands in Iowa, Nebraska, and Kansas were ceded to the United States, which left two of the bands on diminished reservations. One band made up of mostly Fox, which had refused to sign the treaties, joined the Sac and Fox of Iowa and purchased land under the auspices of the General Allotment Act. This act offered individual Native people the chance to acquire portions, or allotments, of land that had previously belonged to the entire tribe. Following the allotment of lands to Indian individual owners, the remaining tribal land was opened to non-Indian settlement. One major effect of allotment was the breaking up of tribal homelands.

The Sac and Fox in Kansas were forced to accept individual allotments. Under the terms of the Treaty of 1867, many people sold their Kansas lands and moved to a reservation in Indian Territory. Some Sac and Fox remained in Kansas. Those who left Kansas moved to Indian Territory in 1869. Many of those who had stayed in Kansas were ravaged by disease and death, and the remaining Sac and Fox were eventually removed to Indian Territory under escort of the United States Cavalry in 1886.

In the spring of 1885, the Sauk and the Fox formally organized the Sac and Fox Nation with a written constitution and laws that were adopted and later published. The constitution provided for tribal courts, which had jurisdiction within the reservation.

In June 1890, the Sac and Fox ceded their reservation lands in Indian Territory to the United States and were forced to accept individual allotments. The surplus lands were opened up for settlement by a land run that began at noon, September 22, 1891.

The Sac and Fox reorganized under the Oklahoma Indian Welfare Act of 1936. They are currently headquartered in Stroud, Oklahoma. Today, the Sac and Fox are still concerned with issues of tribal rights and are known for standing up for their rights as a sovereign nation. They are enterprising and have found many industrious ways to bring employment to their people.

SEE ALSO:

Black Hawk; General Allotment Act; Illinois; Kansas; Oklahoma; Tecumseh; Thorpe, Grace; Thorpe, Jim.

SACAJAWEA (c. 1784–1812)

As a teenager with a two-month-old baby on a cradleboard strapped to her back, Sacajawea (Bird Woman) helped guide the Lewis and Clark expedition for nineteen months over the Rocky Mountains toward the Pacific Coast near today's Astoria, Oregon. Without Sacajawea's skill with languages, her familiarity with various Native peoples, and her knowledge of forest trails and edible plants, the expedition may well have halted on several occasions. The exact role that Sacajawea played in the expedition has been the subject of some debate among historians. Some, such as David Hurst Thomas in *The Native Americans: An Illustrated History* (1993), write that Sacajawea embodied the qualities of several people but that she did, as an interpreter and bridge between different cultures, "help [the expedition] at critical points."

Sacajawea was born among the Lemhi Shoshone in Idaho. When she was ten, Hidatsa Indians kidnapped her during a raid and took her to a village in present-day North Dakota. In 1804, Sacajawea was won or purchased by Toussaint Charbonneau, a French-Canadian trader.

In 1803, President Thomas Jefferson had sent Meriwether Lewis and William Clark across the continent with explicit instructions to learn as much as they could about the peoples, plants, and animals along their way. The United States was in the process of obtaining Louisiana, a territory that included much of the present-day Midwest, from France. Lewis and Clark hired Charbonneau for this first transcontinental expedition, and he insisted that Sacajawea go along. Sacajawea had reasons of her own for going: She hoped to be reunited with the Shoshones during the expedition.

Her presence on the expedition was crucial; she translated Shoshone into Hidatsa for Charbonneau, who translated it into English; at times, she used sign language. Sacajawea also saved the expedition's important records when her boat turned over. And she partially achieved her own desire, a surprise reunion with her brother Cameahwait, chief of his band of Shoshones, who saw her at Three Forks of the Missouri River in present-day Montana. Her brother gave horses to the expedition and lent them an elderly Shoshone guide. Despite all her services, Charbonneau was the one paid at the end of the expedition, not Sacajawea.

Little was known of Sacajawea by European-Americans other than Lewis and Clark until 1811, when she and Charbonneau traveled to St. Louis, where Clark had become a regional superintendent

Sacajawea, shown here in a heroic pose that is representative of the way she has often been portrayed by non-Native illustrators, is one of the best-recognized Indian figures in U.S. history.

of Indian affairs. Sacajawea and her husband were visiting St. Louis to accept an offer by Clark to educate their son "Pomp," of whom Clark had become fond during the expedition. Clark's papers note that Sacajawea died shortly after that visit, but some argue that Sacajawea returned to the Shoshones and lived to be almost a hundred years old.

The source of the confusion seems to have been the non-Indian world's later realization that Charbonneau (unknown to Clark) had two Shoshone wives. An argument has been made that the wife who died was not Sacajawea, but Otter Woman, his other wife. Various historians cite accounts of Sacajawea that see her into old age; others assert that Clark knew Sacajawea well enough not to mistake her for another woman. This controversy has added to Sacajawea's renown and to the interest taken in her life and deeds. Today, her fame has by far eclipsed that of her husband, the man who was paid for much of the work she accomplished on the Lewis and Clark expedition.

SEE ALSO:

Lewis and Clark Expedition; Louisiana Purchase; Shoshone; Sign Language, Native; Siouan Languages.

SACRED SITES

From ancient times through the present, various Native American cultures, like most cultures, have maintained special places that they consider to be sacred or of special spiritual value. Native people believe that these sacred sites, many of which are located outdoors, were chosen by the Creator as specific places to perform specific religious ceremonies or to serve as burial grounds. The fact that these sites are outdoors, in nature, has led to many abuses by non-Indians who do not understand the spiritual significance of holy places that are not enclosed by four walls and topped with a steeple.

When the U.S. government removed Indians from their ancestral homelands in the 1800s, many people were forced to leave sacred places where they had conducted their ceremonies for centuries. When, for example, settlers found gold and other valuable resources in the Black Hills of South Dakota, land that is sacred to the Sioux people was tramped on by outsiders and ultimately taken from the Indians so it could be mined. In the view of most Native people, this type of action amounts to the desecration of a sacred site, just as bulldozing such sites as Calvary (the hill where Christ is said to have been crucified), the Western Wall (the remains of the old Temple in Jerusalem), or the Dome of the Rock (where Muhammad is said to have ascended into Heaven) and drilling to get the oil underneath would be a desecration of Christian, Jewish, and Muslim holy sites in modern-day Israel.

Like the Black Hills in Sioux country, Mount Graham in Arizona is sacred to the San Carlos Apaches. The University of Arizona, in its plan to build an observatory on top of Mount Graham, was originally going to name the large telescope the "Columbus Project," but because of the sensitive issues of building the observatory on sacred Indian land and the offense that most Indian people would take to naming it after Christopher Columbus, the name was changed. In the minds of many critics of the project, the fact that it is being funded largely through the United States government adds insult to the injury of the entire enterprise. The government has a long history of disregarding the Native cultures whose lands and traditions stand in the way of settlements, roads, buildings, and other projects built in the name of progress and the national interest.

Other incursions by non-Native enterprises have destroyed or endangered sacred Indian sites. For example, an electric company in Tennessee built a dam and flooded the ancestral homelands of Cherokee people living in the area. Not only did many have to give up their homes, but ancient burial grounds were also flooded. Throughout North America, Indian mounds and burial grounds have been opened and turned into sites of archaeological digs. Despite Native religions' strict rules about burials and the violation of burial sites, most items found in these burial grounds have been placed in museums. Recent legislation has ordered the return of many of these items—including the bones of ancestors—to their rightful tribal sources for proper reburial and repatriation.

Throughout the continent, burial grounds have been covered by water, golf courses, and even discount stores. In some cases, where there was no archaeological or scientific interest in the grave sites, developers and contractors have disregarded the remains of ancient ones completely, effectively turning those remains into filler for highways. When cases such as these are taken to court—like others in which developers run their equipment over Indian graves—the rulings against Indian nations (and their spiritual beliefs) are often based on the supremacy of the government's interest in the land.

In 1994, the Native American Freedom of Religion Act was sent to Congress. This act would allow the ritual use of eagle feathers, religious freedom for prisoners, the use of peyote in ceremonies, and the right to other religious practices that have been denied Indian people. The bill also allows for the protection of sacred sites.

This act did not pass Congress. One stumbling block to its passage was the sacred sites section, which held that Indian nations had to report the locations of all their sacred sites in order to gain protection for the sites. Many Indian-rights activists, who understand that in many Native religions sacred sites are not to be discussed , objected to that provision.

Another problem that Indian-rights people have with the bill is the fact that, even when the sites are known and under protection, the federal government would still have the right to desecrate the site if it was deemed to be in the national interest to do so. And in the past, the courts have consistently upheld the government's position on this point as Indian nations have watched their most sacred places become violated.

Many people are still working on the wording

A handmade cross graces the landscape of the Tohono O'odham Reservation. For many Native people, a piece of land need not have a church on it to have spiritual significance.

of the act in the hope that Indian nations and the United States can come to some agreement. In the meantime, the sites remain unprotected.

SEE ALSO:

Black Hills; Mount Graham Observatory; Native American Graves Protection and Repatriation Act; Reburial and Repatriation of Human Remains and Sacred Objects; Removal Act, Indian.

SAINTE-MARIE, BUFFY (1942–)

Buffy Sainte-Marie is a well-known Cree singer, composer, and American Indian rights activist. She is devoted to her musical talents and her Native heritage and has brought together these two passions as a way to carry vital and triumphant messages to people everywhere.

Buffy Sainte-Marie was born on February 20, 1942, on the Piapot Indian Reserve at Craven, Saskatchewan. Her parents, who were both Cree Indians, died when she was just a few months old.

She came to live in the United States in Massachusetts and Maine after she was adopted by Albert and Winifred Sainte-Marie, both part Micmac.

As a child growing up, Buffy Sainte-Marie often spent long, solitary hours wandering in the woods near her home, writing poems and making up simple tunes. It wasn't until she was seventeen years old that she was given her first guitar. After finishing high school, she attended the University of Massachusetts, where she majored in Oriental philosophy and education and was named one of the ten outstanding seniors in her class. Her plans were to teach after graduation, but the positive response to her folksinging on her college campus made her consider her future differently.

In 1963, Sainte-Marie visited New York City and began singing in folk clubs such as the Gaslight Cafe, the Bitter End, and Gerde's Folk City in Greenwich Village. She soon caught the attention of an agent and began appearing in coffeehouses, nightclubs, and concerts as well as producing a series of best-selling albums. By 1967, Sainte-Marie had become an international star and gave concerts in Lincoln Center and Carnegie Hall in New York, in the Royal Albert Hall in London, at Montreal's Expo 67, and on many stages in Canada, Mexico, and Europe.

Buffy Sainte-Marie owes much of her success to her dramatic vocal delivery and strong presence on stage. She usually accompanies herself on guitar or with an American Indian instrument called a mouthbow, which is one of the oldest musical instruments in the world. Her song repertoire has

Surrounded by a group of young traditional dancers from the Six Nations Reserve in Ontario, famed Cree singer and composer Buffy Sainte-Marie accepts an award in 1995.

included traditional folk songs in addition to material written by other contemporary composers. Primarily, however, Sainte-Marie records and performs music she has composed herself, including city blues, country tunes, love ballads, and protest songs. She is most widely recognized for her protest songs, songs such as "Now That the Buffalo's Gone," "My Country 'Tis of Thy People You're Dying," and "Universal Soldier." These songs give voice to her commitment to the fight for Indian rights and to the antiwar protest movement of the 1960s. One of her most recent recordings is *Confidence and Likely Stories*, recorded in 1992.

In addition to her successful musical career, Buffy Sainte-Marie is also a writer and a lecturer whose speaking out on behalf of Indian and other human rights has taken her to Western Europe, Canada, and Mexico. She also has done some acting, appearing in the television series *The Virginian* in 1968. She has been published in *The Native Voice, Thunderbird, American Indian Horizons*, and *Boston Broadside* and has also written a children's book entitled *Nokosis and the Magic Hat* (1986).

SAINT REGIS/AKWESASNE MOHAWKS

SEE Akwesasne (St. Regis Reservation), Pollution of.

SAMOSET (c. 1590–c. 1653)

Samoset, whose name means "He Who Walks over Much" in the Abenaki language, made contact with English fishermen near the home of his band, the Pemaquid Abenakis, on Monhegan Island off the coast of Maine. Samoset had learned enough from the fishermen so that by the time the Pilgrims reached the area that later became known as New England in 1620, he was able to greet them in English. On March 21, 1621, he surprised the English immigrants by walking into Plymouth Plantation (in present-day Massachusetts) and announcing, "Welcome, Englishmen!" Samoset was nearly naked despite freezing weather; the settlers gave him clothing and food, and they became friendly.

Samoset creates a stir among a group of surprised Pilgrims as he strolls into their Plymouth settlement on March 21, 1621. This 1876 engraving portrays the colonists as ranging from moderate dismay to intense curiosity in their presumed reactions to his presence.

Samoset returned to the Plymouth settlement on March 22 in the company of Squanto, who had also learned English. (Squanto had been taken hostage by Europeans, sent to Spain and later to England, and returned to America, all before the Pilgrims reached Plymouth.) Samoset and Squanto arranged a meeting between the colonists and the Wampanoags' principal chief, Massasoit. This meeting was the beginning of Massasoit's long-term friendship with the New England settlers.

During the first years of European settlement, Samoset "sold" large tracts of land at the Pilgrims' urgent request. He acknowledged the first such deed in 1625 for 12,000 acres (4,800 hectares) of Pemaquid territory.

SEE ALSO:
Abenaki; Maine; Massachusetts; Massasoit; Squanto; Wampanoag.

SAN CARLOS RESERVATION

The San Carlos Apache Reservation consists of 1.9 million acres (760,000 hectares) in eastern Arizona, with tribal headquarters at San Carlos, Arizona. Its population is more than six thousand. San Carlos Reservation and the adjacent Fort Apache Reservation were one unit until they were administratively divided in 1897. In the 1920s, the San Carlos Apaches established a business committee, which was dominated by the Bureau of Indian Affairs (BIA). The business committee evolved into a tribal council, which now runs the tribe as a corporation.

Many Apache children were sent to the Carlisle Indian School in Pennsylvania not long after the school was founded in 1879 by Richard Henry Pratt; a large group of children arrived in 1887. Government and mission schools were established among the Apaches in the 1890s. These schools

Peridot, Arizona, a town on the San Carlos Apache Reservation, lies on San Carlos Lake in the shadow of the Gila Mountains. In this photo, the three points of Triplet Peak loom in the distance.

Mountain Spirit dancers on the San Carlos Apache Reservation, often referred to as Crown Dancers, perform healing rites and other ceremonies. Mountain Spirit masks are usually made of buckskin hoods that are painted black, fitted tightly over the head, and drawn around the neck with a string.

vigorously pursued policies that forced Indians to assimilate to the dominant culture, including instruction in English only. By 1952, 80 percent of the Apaches in Arizona spoke English. Today, Apaches participate in decisions involving the education of their young, resulting in exemplary bilingual and bicultural programs at the public schools at both the San Carlos and Fort Apache Reservations, especially in the elementary grades.

By 1925, the Bureau of Indian Affairs had leased nearly all of the San Carlos Reservation to non-Indian cattlemen, who demonstrated no concern about overgrazing. The reservation also lost most of its best farmland when Coolidge Dam was completed in 1930 and the reservation's lands were flooded. Recreational concessions around the lake mostly benefited non-Natives.

By the end of the 1930s, the tribe regained control of its rangeland, and most San Carlos Apaches became stockmen. Today, the San Carlos Apache cattle operation generates more than one million dollars annually in sales. Cattle, timber, and mining leases provide other revenue. There is some individual mining activity for the semiprecious

peridot gemstones. Despite the tribe's business successes, however, more than 50 percent of the tribe is unemployed. A chronically high level of unemployment is the norm on most reservations in the United States.

At the southern end of the reservation, Mt. Graham, 10,720 feet (3,252 meters) in elevation, is sacred land to the Apaches. It is currently threatened by a controversial project of the University of Arizona to destroy the natural habitat on the mountaintop and replace it with a celestial observatory.

Gift shops selling locally made traditional crafts can be found at visitor centers, museums, or the tribal complex on the Apache reservations in Arizona and New Mexico. San Carlos Apache women are famous for their twined burden baskets made in full size and in miniature. Another specialty is coiled basketry, featuring complex designs in black devil's claw.

The San Carlos Apaches perform the Sunrise Dance and Mountain Spirit Dance throughout the summer, but their traditional dances are most easily observed at the San Carlos Tribal Fair, which is celebrated annually over Labor Day weekend. The San Carlos Apaches maintain four campgrounds on their reservation, at Cassadore Springs, Cienega Park, Point of Pines, and San Carlos Marina.

SEE ALSO:

Apache; Arizona; Bureau of Indian Affairs; Carlisle Indian School; Fort Apache Reservation; Mount Graham Observatory; New Mexico.

SAND CREEK MASSACRE

On November 29, 1864, the United States Cavalry, led by John Chivington, approached Indian lodges housing two hundred men and about five hundred women and children along Sand Creek in eastern Colorado. Of the one hundred lodges, ten were under Arapaho Chief Left Hand and the others under Cheyenne Chiefs Black Kettle, White Antelope, and other peace chiefs.

The soldiers had marched all night and reached the lodges at dawn. Some women saw the soldiers and were assured of their safety. Black Kettle ran a U.S. flag and a white flag up a pole outside his tipi as a sign of friendship.

The cavalry then opened fire on the unsuspecting Indians, who tried to run away. They ran up the dry stream and tried to hide in sandpits, but the soldiers followed and fired into the pits. When White Antelope refused to run and stood singing his death song, the soldiers shot and killed him. Children were shot climbing out of sandpits and waving white flags. Mothers carrying babies were shot down. The soldiers finally stopped firing and went back to the lodges and mutilated the bodies of the dead; they took more than one hundred scalps of Indian people and displayed them in Denver, where the soldiers were upheld as "heroes." Among the dead Cheyennes were nine of their leading chiefs.

The seeds of what would come to be known as the Sand Creek Massacre had been planted in 1861. That year, the Cheyennes had signed a treaty that confined them to a small reservation in Colorado. There were rumors that the Indians were planning a full-scale war, but these rumblings were started among the settlers and soldiers. In addition to these stories, rumors of cattle raids by Indians were also reported, but investigations found no evidence of any truth to these reports.

Troops of soldiers were sent to discipline the "hostile" Indians. When the troops fired on the Cheyennes, killing two chiefs, warriors pursued the troops and began raiding their forts. Colonel Chivington—a former Christian preacher who believed he was justified in killing Indian babies because, he said, "nits make lice"—was ordered to kill all Cheyennes and take no prisoners. Major Edward W. Wynkoop took a letter, offering peace, to the chiefs at Smoky Hill. But not all of the warriors agreed to stop what had become a war, and many carried out raids on U.S. forts and on the wagon trails.

The peace chiefs nonetheless agreed to make peace, but the members of the army, who wanted entire tribes to surrender to military authority, would continue their attacks until this wholesale surrender took place. The peace chiefs did not know or understand this theory and left a peace meeting thinking they had agreed to peace. Black Kettle moved his people to Sand Creek because the government had promised to keep them safe there, and it was there, in 1864, that Chivington's troops carried out their massacre.

After the Sand Creek Massacre, Congress conducted an investigation and found a great deal of damning evidence against the military. Children had been beaten to death, and pregnant women had been cut open. Soldiers had mutilated the bodies of the dead to the point where individuals could not be recognized. When made public, massacres such as the one committed at Sand Creek—and, in years to come, other injustices committed against Indians by the United States—gradually began to change non-Indian attitudes toward Indians, eventually chipping away at the one-dimensional image of Native people as hostile or savage.

SEE ALSO:
Arapaho; Black Kettle; Cheyenne; Left Hand, the Elder; Wars, Indian.

SANTEE SIOUX RESISTANCE

SEE Sioux Uprising (1862).

SASKATCHEWAN

Covering 251,866 square miles (654,852 square kilometers), the Canadian province of Saskatchewan is geographically part of the Great Plains of North America. It is bounded by Manitoba on the east, Alberta on the west, the Northwest Territories to the north, and the U.S. states of Montana and North Dakota to the south. The northern region of the province is wooded, with lakes and tundra. Regina is Saskatchewan's capital city, and the province's economy is rooted in agriculture, forestry, and mining.

Saskatchewan's earliest inhabitants were members of Chipewyan, Cree, Dakota (Sioux), Ojibwe (Chippewa), and Assiniboine bands. Most of these First Nations people moved seasonally and practiced a Plains Indian lifestyle. Their economy was based on hunting, fishing, gathering, and trading. They traveled on foot and horseback, using a travois to carry belongings and living in tipis. (A travois is a v-shaped wooden device used to transport people and possessions behind dogs or horses.)

"Rupert's Land," a large area that included modern-day Saskatchewan, was granted to the Hudson's Bay Company in 1670. Many of the Plains tribes became middlemen in the trading of European goods to outlying tribes, trapping furs, and selling pemmican (a concentrated food made by pounding together meat, fat, and berries) to the trading posts. During this era, the Crees dominated the Saskatchewan plains. In the 1800s, the diminishing of buffalo and other big game, population losses due to European diseases, and the completion of a railroad that brought more settlers all combined to dispossess the indigenous peoples of their lands and their way of life.

In 1870, the Hudson's Bay Company transferred "Rupert's Land" to Canada. During the 1870s, the Plains Indians lost most of their lands to the government in return for various "treaty rights." The Métis were not dealt with by treaty and, dispossessed by settlers, they were without hope of compensation. This led to the second Riel Rebellion in

A news photo, taken in 1972, of Jim Sinclair *(left)*, president of the Saskatchewan Métis Society, meeting with Pierre Trudeau, the prime minister of Canada, to discuss decades-old problems with land and treaty issues. The Métis, an indigenous culture with Native and European roots, have long struggled with the Canadian government over issues of land and tribal sovereignty.

Saskatchewan (1885), in which the Métis, under the leadership of Louis Riel and Gabriel Dumont, attempted to establish their rights to their own lands. They were joined by several other bands, including Poundmaker's Cree people. The rebellion was suppressed, and the province of Saskatchewan was created in 1905.

By the turn of the century, most of Saskatchewan's First Nations people were settled on reserves under restrictive provisions and coerced into changing to an agriculture- and ranch-based economy. They began organizing in the 1920s to work for better education, health, and social services and to preserve their treaty rights. The Federation of Saskatchewan Indians became quite influential in the 1930s and 1940s. In 1985, a new alliance was organized as the Prairie Treaty Nations Alliance in order to further efforts in reclaiming treaty rights and fostering self-government. Saskatchewan contains 142 reserves totaling more than 1,514,316 acres (613,298 hectares). In 1986, more than twenty-seven thousand Native people lived on reserves, and more than fifty thousand lived off-reserve in Saskatchewan.

SEE ALSO:

Hudson's Bay Company; Métis; Poundmaker; Riel, Louis.

SAUK

SEE Sac and Fox.

Despite the fact that scalping was primarily a way for non-Indian bounty hunters to collect a reward for killing Native people, illustrations like this promoted the perception of scalping as an act of savagery by Indians against defenseless Euro-American settlers.

SCALPING

Scalping was a practice that has, over time, become more defined by misconceptions, half-truths, and sensational images than by its true role in the history of relations between Native Americans and Euro-Americans.

During colonial times and in the early days of the existence of the United States as an independent nation, scalping—the removal of a portion of the skin covering the top of the human head with its hair attached—was first used by non-Indian traders after a bounty was placed on Indians. (A bounty is a reward or a payment given by the government to people performing acts that are viewed as being for the good of the state, such as killing predatory animals. Often, animal scalps have been accepted as proof of killing for the purpose of collecting a bounty.) At various times in the early history of the United States, official government policy called for the elimination of Indians from lands claimed by the government. One means of eliminating Native people was killing them in great numbers, either through military campaigns or by paying citizens to kill them. Because of the weight of dead bodies, traders found it easier either to skin the Indians or to scalp them after killing them. The traders would then take the scalps to the federal government or to colonists who would pay based on the number of Indians killed. Many Indians were murdered so that traders could collect reward money.

The size of the bounty often depended on the age and gender of the Indian scalped. For example, the scalp of an adult Indian male would be worth more than that of an adult Indian female. The scalp of a boy or a girl was worth less than that of an adult.

Various cultures have, throughout their histories, given a place of honor to warriors who presented scalps or other battle trophies as proof of victory. In the case of relations between Native peoples and non-Native Americans, however, the practice of scalping was almost exclusively used as an incentive to induce Euro-Americans to exterminate Native Americans.

In later years, the association of scalping with Native people shifted, and scalping came to be considered an Indian custom. Even though most Indians did not value white men's scalps, newspapers and local and federal governments promoted the idea of Native people scalping whites as propaganda against the "savage" Indians.

Today, many Americans still view scalping as something done to white settlers by Indians. The misconception is so predominant that it is still taught in many public schools and textbooks, whereas incidents of wholesale brutality toward Indians, such as those documented in the writings and art of Spanish priest Bartolomé de Las Casas, still seem fairly exotic and surprising to most Americans.

On the positive side, fewer schools use Indian mascots than in the past, and fewer still have booster organizations called "Scalphunters" that sell fake scalps in their fund-raising campaigns. Nonetheless, due partly to lingering cowboy-and-Indian imagery in sports and old-style Western books, television shows, movies, and art, it is still difficult for most Americans to shake completely free of the picture—and acceptance—of Native cultures as historically violent and savage.

SEE ALSO:
Hollywood, Indians, and Indian Images; Las Casas, Bartolomé de.

SEATTLE, CHIEF

SEE Chief Seattle.

SELF-DETERMINATION

Self-determination is the idea that tribal communities should determine and manage their own trib-

al affairs, including government, economic development, and social and cultural programs. The term is used to describe the federal government's current approach to Indian affairs.

The U.S. government has not always promoted a policy that recognized the Indians' ability to govern themselves. When Euro-American settlers were fanning out across the continent shortly after the birth of the United States, the U.S. government acknowledged the independent status of Indians and did not interfere with tribal governments. However, as the number of settlers grew, so did the demand for land. The government began to practice an Indian affairs policy that involved relocating tribes, limiting their lands, and assimilating Indians into the European-American way of life. In this way, the government began playing a larger role in Indians' everyday life.

In 1934, the Indian Reorganization Act (also called the Indian New Deal) restored the idea of tribal governments and protected tribal lands. But this was followed by the termination era, when the government promoted a policy that ended nation status for tribes and also ended the government's special "trust" relationships with tribes, in which government land was designated for Indian use, free of interference from state or local government.

Civil rights awareness emerged in the 1950s and emphasized equal and fair treatment of women and minority groups. This growing awareness helped promote changes in Indian policy as well. It wasn't until the 1960s that government policy returned to the recognition of tribes as independent communities.

However, the changing attitude toward Indians wasn't solely the result of the federal government or of society's changing awareness. In 1961, a group of Indian representatives from a number of tribes met with the goal of influencing the direction of Indian policy. The tribes gathered in Chicago and created the "Declaration of Indian Purpose," emphasizing Indians' rights to practice rituals that expressed their customary spiritual and cultural values. The tribes also called for improvements in a variety of government policies and programs. They strongly supported the rights of tribes to participate in their own programs and to solve their own problems.

John Wooden Legs of the Northern Cheyennes chats with U.S. President Lyndon B. Johnson at a reception in 1967. In 1968, Johnson would support Indian self-determination as a step toward greater Native control over Native issues.

In 1960, then–Vice President Richard Nixon greets a group of Paiute dancers in Reno, Nevada. Ten years later, as U.S. president, Nixon would also promote the concept of Indian self-determination in an important address to Congress.

It wasn't until 1968 that the current era of self-determination began. President Lyndon B. Johnson called for an end to the policy of termination and promoted the goal of more constructive Indian programs that supported Indian self-determination and encouraged Indian economic and social equality. The idea was continued with President Richard Nixon, who outlined his self-determination policy proposal in a message to Congress in 1970 as follows: First, tribes could not be terminated without tribal consent; second, tribal governments would take control over planning, implementing, and administering their own federal programs; and finally, tribes would be assisted by the government in becoming economically self-sufficient.

Self-determination covers a wide range of Indian affairs topics. It includes restoring tribes that were terminated by the government during the termination era and establishing tribal governments and forms of government based on custom or constitutional governments by choice of tribal leaders. It promotes enhancing and reviving cultural traditions and developing reservation resources, including timber, minerals, grazing lands, and the people themselves. The ultimate goal of self-determination is to see tribes as self-sufficient communities with a perpetual existence.

Federal support for Indian self-determination includes reaffirmation of the federal trust relationship (see second paragraph of this article) and an end to the debate over termination. The U.S. government has a role in providing the assistance of economic and social programs as well as passing legislation to create programs designed to assist the tribes in achieving their goals.

Self-determination has continued to gain support from the federal government. In 1975, the Indian Self-Determination and Education Assistance Act created legislation permitting tribal governments to take on developing programs and making decisions formerly performed by the Bureau of Indian Affairs (BIA). During the next two decades, the act was amended on several occasions to strengthen the legislation. In 1987, the Self-Governance Demonstration Project was initiated. The project promotes the goal of federal-tribal relations on a government-to-government basis and permits tribes to contract directly with the federal government for funds, bypassing the BIA. Additional legislation extended the project to include more tribes, and, in 1994, legislation passed that made the project permanent.

Self-determination is important in that it supports the most basic exercise of tribal sovereign power. Self-determination not only restores pride to tribal communities, but it also creates a much more efficient method of administering programs. Agency control over tribes often consisted of inexperienced employees making decisions without concern or knowledge of the unique needs of individual tribes. The current government policy permits tribes to use funds to their best benefit by addressing their own needs in everything from economic planning and development to education and health programs, creation and maintenance of tribal law and court systems, and tribal housing.

— P. Rentz

SEE ALSO:
Alaska Native Claims Settlement Act and Amendment; Bureau of Indian Affairs; Indian New Deal (Indian Reorganization Act); Self-Determination Policy; Tribal Sovereignty; Termination Policy; Trust Land.

SELF-DETERMINATION POLICY

The U.S. government's self-determination policy evolved from the idea that Indian nations should have the power to govern themselves and determine their own social and economic future. During the 1950s, the government had inflicted the termination policy on Indian tribes, trying to end their status as distinct nations, and attempted to end its special relationship with tribes. But toward the end of the 1950s, people became more aware of civil rights for all people, including women and minority groups. Society's shifting awareness was reflected in changes in Indian policy.

In 1968 in a message to Congress, President Lyndon Johnson introduced new goals for Indian programs. He encouraged an end to termination of Indian programs and, instead, introduced a plan of self-determination, promoting the ideal that tribes should resume control over planning and administering their own programs. He believed that Indian people should be given the opportunity to make their own choices about the future.

Two years later, President Richard Nixon defined his self-determination policy in a message to Congress. He also announced an end to termination of tribal status and asked Congress to officially reject this policy. He reaffirmed the importance of the federal government's trust responsibility to tribes and asked Congress for legislation that would lend strength to this trust responsibility by giving tribes the authority to operate their own federal programs on land that the government designated for Indian use. In addition, Nixon's policy assisted tribes with their own economic development and created programs to assist Indian living in urban areas.

The policy of self-determination is the official policy today. Congress has passed a number of acts to help support self-determination, including legislation regarding education, financial assistance, child welfare, gaming, and the Alaska Native Claims Settlement Act, which granted 44 million acres (17.6 million hectares) and $962 million to Alaskan Natives.

SEE ALSO:
Alaska Native Claims Settlement Act and Amendment; Self-determination; Termination Policy; Tribal Sovereignty; Trust Land.

SELF-GOVERNANCE, TRIBAL

SEE Governments, Native; Self-determination; Self-determination Policy; Tribal Sovereignty.

SEMINOLE

As the Creek Nation was forced from their lands by the arrival of European settlers, a number migrated to Florida. The British called these people the Seminole Creek or Seminole, a name that is derived from a Muscogee Creek word meaning "runaway."

As the colonists pushed westward and southward from their base on the East Coast, many Indian nations moved from the area, among them the Oconee Seminole, who had lived in Georgia since the 1600s. They moved to Florida—land that was

A scene from the Second Seminole War in Florida, which lasted between 1835 and 1842. The battle depicted in this illustration, the first of the conflict, was fought over the forced removal of Seminoles to Indian Territory (present-day Oklahoma) at the hands of U.S. soldiers.

considered neutral territory by the French and English. Also among the nations that moved to this neutral territory were the Yamasee, Apalachicola, Yuchi, and others—the origins of the Seminole Nation. For a time, the Seminoles remained a part of the Creek Confederacy, but, being separated from their people, they eventually became an independent tribe.

The Seminoles became known as the Mikasuki, meaning "Warrior" or "Red Stick" because they were bitterly opposed to any dealings with colonial interests—not the Spanish, French, or English—and after the founding of the United States, not with U.S. interests, either. After the Red Stick War of 1813 to 1814, when the Creeks rebelled against the United States' influence over the leaders of the Creek Council, the Seminole Nation tripled in size with refugees from Creek towns. Black slaves who had managed to run away from their Spanish masters also found refuge among the

Seminoles and eventually formed a large portion of the population.

When Georgia became a state, escaped Black slaves became a source of trouble between white settlers and Indians. Georgia slave owners armed themselves and went into Seminole territory in search of their slaves, thus provoking the First Seminole War between white settlers and Seminoles between 1817 and 1819. General Andrew Jackson invaded Florida (which was still under Spanish rule) with nearly three thousand United States troops, who attacked and burned the town of Mikasuki.

When, following Jackson's incursions into Florida, Spain ceded Florida to the United States in 1810, many U.S. citizens—particularly those from Georgia who had fought against the Seminoles—demanded the removal of the Seminoles from the fertile lands where they lived to another part of the state. The Seminoles were forced off their farmlands and into the Florida swamps; for many, near starvation was the result. The tribe also continued to endure raids conducted by Euro-American men seeking their slaves, permission for which had been granted by the United States War Department.

The Indian Removal Act of May 1830 was signed by President Andrew Jackson; it called for removal of the so-called Five Civilized Tribes living in the Southeast, including the Seminoles, to Indian Territory in today's Oklahoma. This act was followed by forced treaties with eastern tribes to cede their lands and accept reservations in Indian Territory. Seven Seminole signers to the treaty of 1832 that ceded Seminole land took a scouting party west to find a reserve location in the Creek Nation. They were accompanied by John Phagan, who was the federal government's agent, and an interpreter, a Black man named Abraham. The seven— John Blunt, John Hicks, Holahte Emathla, Charley Emathla, and Jumper—arrived in Fort Gibson, Indian Territory, in November 1832. They reported to their people in Florida that the western country was good, but they objected to settling near the Indians of the Plains. Jumper was particularly opposed to settling near the "roguish" Plains tribes.

While the delegation was visiting Creek country, the United States instructed commissioners to secure a treaty with the Creek Nation that would settle the boundary lines of the Creek reservation and would also make the Seminoles part of the Creek Nation. The agreement also allowed the commissioners to settle the Seminoles in a part of the land to be selected by the commissioners. Agent Phagan managed to get the delegation to sign an agreement on April 12, 1833, even though some of the delegation were not authorized to enter into treaty negotiations.

A contemporary Seminole woman prepares food for guests at a get-together near Tampa, Florida.

Many of the Seminoles in Florida were concerned with being merged with the Creek Nation, and most were also opposed to settling into a new country where they could be drawn into wars among other tribes, particularly the Plains nations. The Seminoles refused to recognize the treaty and urged Phagan to call a council, but he refused. He told them that all the Seminoles had to leave Florida. Chief John Blunt and his followers left Florida, and Phagan was later removed from office because of his handling of tribal funds.

According to the treaties, the Seminoles were supposed to remove themselves from Florida in 1835, and a few tribal leaders agreed to depart in late fall and early winter of that year. Opposition to this plan arose among the Seminoles, who were

A picturesque setting in the Florida swamp. Florida Seminoles are closely tied to the state's tourism industry—a somewhat ironic relationship, considering the fact that the tribe never officially surrendered to the United States at the end of the so-called Seminole Wars of the 1800s.

influenced by Osceola and other leaders. Charley Emathla, who had signed the treaty agreeing to the removal, was killed, along with General A. R. Thompson, who had tried to force the tribe to leave. The U.S. agent then told the Seminoles that, if they were not ready to leave Florida on the set date, U.S. troops would be sent in to enforce the removal. He and other government employees were killed by a band of warriors led by Osceola. The same day, December 28, 1835, a party of Seminoles and their African-American allies attacked and killed all but three of a company of 110 U.S. soldiers on their way to Ocala, Florida, to aide in the removal process.

The campaign against the Seminoles increased when the government was not able to conquer them. Towns and provisions were burned and destroyed, cattle were killed, and horses taken. Former slaves were captured and told they would gain freedom if they tracked the Indians. Seminole families hid deep within the swamps, while the war-riors successfully kept the U.S. troops at bay. Under a flag of truce, Osceola was captured with Wild Cat, the son of Seminole chief King Phillip. Wild Cat managed to escape prison, but Osceola could not. He later died there, many say of a "broken spirit."

By the end of this Second Seminole War in 1842, the Seminole people of Florida had successfully held off the United States and removal for seven years. The war against the Seminoles had cost the United States fifteen hundred soldiers and approximately $20 million. By war's end, the federal government agreed that several hundred Seminoles could stay in Florida under certain conditions. They stayed in the swamps but never surrendered.

As other leaders surrendered, they were sent to Indian Territory, where they arrived poor, sick, and dying. Wild Cat never accepted rule under the Creek Nation. He left in 1850 to start a Seminole colony in Mexico, across the Rio Grande from Eagle Pass, Texas.

Plans to settle the Seminoles on land ceded by the Creek Nation were disrupted by the U.S. Civil War. Like many Indian nations, particularly those that now lived in Indian Territory, the Seminoles were split by the Union and the Confederacy, with different tribal factions fighting on opposite sides of the conflict.

By 1868, the Seminoles who moved to Indian Territory, known as the "Seminole Nation," were settled in their own area after having bought land from the Creek Nation. They made their capital in Wewoka, Indian Territory, and erected their council house. Their government consists today of a principal chief, second chief, a national council, and a company of light horsemen (police).

The Seminoles concentrate on education for their youth and on profitable business ventures to ensure sovereignty for their people. The Seminoles who still live on reservations in the southern part of Florida, although smaller in number than their Oklahoma counterparts, are highly visible and have made a living catering to Florida's tourist business. Seminole "Indian villages" have long been a popular draw for visitors lured by various festivals and the spectacle of alligator "wrestling" exhibitions. More important, however, is the perpetuation of the Seminoles' tribal art, economy, identity, and way of life in these villages.

— S. S. Davis

SEE ALSO:
Civil War, U.S., Indians in; Creek; Five Civilized Tribes; Florida; Oklahoma; Osceola; Removal Act, Indian.

SUGGESTED READINGS:

Debo, Angie. A History of the Indians of the United States. Norman: University of Oklahoma Press, 1970.

Wright, Muriel H. A Guide to the Indian Tribes of Oklahoma. Norman: University of Oklahoma Press, 1951.

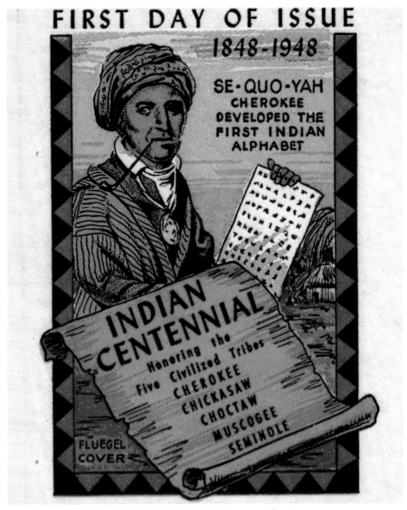

This illustration of Cherokee scholar Sequoyah decorates an envelope honoring the first day of issue of a stamp commemorating the so-called Indian Centennial of Oklahoma (formerly Indian Territory) in 1948.

SEQUOYAH (c. 1760–1843)

Sequoyah (also spelled Sequoya; in Cherokee, Sikwayi; and in English, George Gist, Guess, or Guest) was a mixed-blood Cherokee scholar who is credited with creating the Cherokee language writing system in the early nineteenth century. He was born around 1760 near Fort Loudon on the Tennessee River, and he died between 1843 and 1845 near San Fernando, Tamaulipas, Mexico.

Sequoyah was the son of a Cherokee woman, Wurteh, and a British trader, probably Nathaniel Gist, who abandoned Wurteh during her pregnancy. Early in life, Sequoyah was known as an accomplished hunter and trapper, and later in life, he gained a reputation as a silversmith, craftsman, and artist. Sequoyah served in a Cherokee division of the United States Army during the War of 1812 and the Creek wars of 1813–1814.

Sequoyah spent much of his life on the move to avoid the intrusion of white men into Indian lands. Born in Tennessee, he moved early in his life to Alabama, and in 1818, he moved to Arkansas with a group of Cherokees led by Chief John Jolly. The time that Sequoyah did spend in the company of white people, including his military service, led him to believe that writing, or what he referred to as "talking leaves," was a source of white power. Sequoyah became convinced that if the Cherokee people could learn to read and write in their own language, they could maintain their independence from European-Americans.

In 1821, Sequoyah completed a Cherokee syllabary that comprised eighty-six symbols, each representing one syllable of the Cherokee language. Sequoyah taught his system to his daughter, and together they traveled from Arkansas to the Eastern Cherokee homelands to demonstrate his invention at the Cherokee National Council at Echota, Georgia. When he was able to teach some Cherokee men how to use his "talking leaves" to read and write, the council sanctioned his invention for the whole nation.

Because of the basic simplicity of Sequoyah's system, the ability to read and write spread rapidly among the Eastern Cherokee. Sequoyah returned west in 1822 and taught the Western Cherokee his system. For the first time, the two groups were able to communicate with each other in writing. The writing system was taught in Cherokee schools; books, including the Bible, were translated into Cherokee for the first time; and in 1828, a weekly newspaper in Cherokee and English, the *Cherokee Phoenix*, began publication.

In 1828, Sequoyah was part of a Western Cherokee delegation to Washington, D.C., that ceded their land in Arkansas for land in what is now Sequoyah County, Oklahoma. The Western Cherokees were joined in the Indian Territory (present-day Oklahoma) in the late 1830s by the survivors of the forced march of Cherokees from their eastern homeland to the territory; that march is known as the Cherokee Trail of Tears. In 1839, Sequoy-

ah helped to mediate a series of violent disputes between the diverse Cherokee factions. In 1842, he set out to find a Cherokee band that had, according to tradition, moved west of the Mississippi River before the American Revolution. It was on this journey that he met his death in Mexico sometime between 1843 and 1845. There is a statue of Sequoyah in Washington, D.C., to honor his accomplishments, and the giant redwood trees of northern California, the sequoias, are named after him.

SEE ALSO:

Cherokee; Cherokee Alphabet; *Cherokee Phoenix*; Oklahoma; Trail of Tears.

SERPENT MOUND

The Great Serpent Mound of Ohio is an example of what archaeologists call an effigy mound, a mound of earth fashioned into the shape of an animal or a bird. It is also believed to be the largest such mound still in existence, measuring 1,130 feet (343 meters) long. The mound is about 20 feet (6 meters) wide and varies from 2 to 5 feet (61 to 152 centimeters) in height. Its purpose is a mystery.

The Great Serpent Mound was probably constructed by an ancient people of the North American continent whom archaeologists have named the Adena Culture. The center of the Adena Culture was in the Ohio River Valley. The culture reached its peak by about 100 B.C.E. The Adena were the earliest mound builders, and they were succeeded by another mound-builder culture called Hopewell, who in turn were succeeded by another culture of mound builders known as the Mississippian Culture.

The Mississippian Culture was still flourishing when Europeans first began exploring the North American continent. The de Soto expedition, in particular, noted several locations in the Southeast where the culture was still being practiced. Thus, the Adena were an early part of a long series of Eastern Woodlands cultures that formed and shaped the earth into mounds.

The Adena constructed many different types of mounds. Most Adena mounds were simple bur-

The Great Serpent Mound threads its way through the landscape of southern Ohio in this dramatic aerial photo. No one knows for sure the precise purpose or meaning of this mound to its ancient builders, but it is believed to be the largest serpent mound still in existence.

ial mounds. Many others, however, consist of a wide variety of geometric patterns that seem to be enclosures.

Some Adena mounds are quite large, the largest standing sixty-eight feet (over twenty meters) high. The most intriguing type of mound, however, is the effigy mound. Many of these shapes, such as birds, or the Great Serpent Mound, are only fully appreciated when viewed from the air. Though the Great Serpent Mound, in southwestern Ohio, is the largest extant effigy mound, there is a large concentration of effigy mounds in present-day Wisconsin, and other effigy mounds have been found throughout the core area of Adena Culture in the Ohio River valley. It is doubtful that anyone will ever know for sure what their purpose might have been or why so much labor was expended for their construction.

The Great Serpent Mound has been repeatedly threatened by commercial development schemes throughout the twentieth century. Its setting, in a lovely valley along Brush Creek, is still relatively undisturbed, but only because of vigorous opposition campaigns against despoiling the area. The most recent proposed scheme, in 1994, would have built a dam on Brush Creek to create a lake to accompany a golf course, an amusement park, and a suburban residential community. A national campaign was organized to fight the proposed development by people who believe that the Great Serpent Mound should remain undisturbed in its natural environment. They succeeded in stopping the project.

SEE ALSO:
Adena Culture; De Soto Expedition; Hopewell Culture; Mississippian Culture; Mound Builders.

SHAKOPEE

The name Shakopee (meaning "Six") was shared by several nineteenth-century Mdewakanton Sioux leaders, whose village was located along the Minnesota River on the site where the town of Shakopee was later constructed. Shakopee the Elder died in 1862, on the eve of the great Sioux Uprising in Minnesota, after having spent his life trying to promote peace between Indians and Euro-Americans. He had signed the Traverse des Sioux Treaty in 1851 and, in 1858, had traveled to Washington, D.C., seeking reconciliation.

Shakopee's son of the same name (who was often called "Little Six" by whites) joined Little Crow in the Sioux Uprising and fled to Canada after the rebellion was crushed. Shakopee escaped the mass hanging at Mankato, Minnesota, that followed the uprising, but he and Medicine Bottle were kidnapped from Canada in 1864 by Major Edwin Hatch, act-ing on orders from General Henry Hastings Sibley. Both men were returned to the United States, quickly tried, sentenced to death, and hanged.

In the 1980s, the Mdewakanton Sioux established a prosperous casino and named it Little Six, after Shakopee the Younger.

SEE ALSO:
Little Crow; Siouan Nations; Sioux Uprising (1862).

SHAMANISM

The word *shaman* has long caused controversy among many Native people and others. Many indigenous people associate the word with anthropologists who are insensitive to Native cultures, non-Natives who think they know a lot about Native spirituality, or non-Natives who are ignorant of Native Americans'

John and Tina Quilt and their children stand outside their home in Prior Lake, Minnesota. A member of the Shakopee Mdewakanton Sioux, Tina Quilt traces her cultural roots back through several generations of Mdewakanton leaders named Shakopee.

feelings. Indigenous people refer to their own holy people and curers by other terms—doctor, medicine person, spiritual leader, elder, herbalist, or diagnostician—thus recognizing a wide variety of callings and skills.

Before the term *shaman* became popular in anthropological writings, indigenous healers and religious persons were often referred to as "witch doctors," "sorcerers," or other terms that carried derogatory or disrespectful overtones. But shaman is not an innocent term either, because it rises out of a clear misunderstanding of, and denigration of, non-European cultures.

According to *Merriam-Webster's New Collegiate Dictionary* (1993 edition), the word refers to "a priest or priestess who uses magic for the purpose of curing the sick, divining the hidden, and controlling events." The dictionary goes on to define shamanism as "characterized by belief in an unseen world of gods, demons, and ancestral spirits responsive only to shamans; also: any similar religion."

In the view of some critics, these definitions present a culturally hostile picture since terms such as *magic, demons, gods*, and *ancestral spirits* are often interpreted as backward, evil, or even "devilish" by many non-Native readers. Moreover, shamanistic religions have usually been regarded as more "primitive" than other religions by people who feel that religious systems must "evolve" or "progress" in order to keep up with changing times and needs. Such a loosely applied picture of shamans and shamanism is also troubling to many Native people since there are some systems of Native spirituality, especially among the Inuit, that *are* shamanistic. One feature of such a system is the soul flight, or spirit flight, in which the shaman goes into a trance, leaves the body, and may thus make contact with powers beyond the everyday world.

All of this is complicated today by a new generation of European-Americans and Europeans who not only are promoting the idea of Native American shamanism but wish to become shamans themselves or study under shamans. These shamans are

An undated photo portraying a healer caring for a sick man. The camera, often intrusive, was especially so on such a sacred occasion, as is shown by the look on the patient's face. This photo was probably used to promote tourism in the Pacific Northwest.

mostly non-Native, but a few are of Native background. Magazines, such as *Shaman's Drum* and *Wildfire* to name two, promote shamanism, while others promote witchcraft and various "pagan" revivals. All of a sudden, shamanism has become fashionable with New Age adherents and others who are drawn to non-European symbols and rituals (especially Native American and Tibetan, but with concepts also liberally borrowed from Hindu philosophy and from other non-Western traditions that may be easily appropriated).

But a look at so-called shamanism from a multicultural perspective instead of a Eurocentric one suggests that many "shamans" are actually non-

A contemporary sweat lodge typical of the kind used by Indians of the Plains for spiritual and healing ceremonies. Like many spiritual traditions, including the performance of healing by holy people, the use of a sweat lodge has been appropriated by many non-Native people in an attempt to practice "authentic" Native religion.

Indian religious leaders who have their own kind of "magic" that they draw upon. Some argue that the most famous shamans of the twentieth century have been non-Native people like Amy Semple McPherson (founder of the Foursquare Church), evangelist Oral Roberts, and the legendary Presbyterian evangelist Billy Sunday. Moreover, the day-to-day work of shamanism in North America is carried on by a variety of religious leaders. Roman Catholic and other priests daily enact rituals that may be viewed as shamanistic, such as Mass, a "magic" ritual in which wine becomes blood and wafers become flesh. Charismatic Protestant preachers and healers attempt to cure by the laying on of the hands and other techniques of faith healing, and religious figures (preachers or priests) attempt to "control" events, obtain wealth, drive away death, or determine who gets into "heaven" by means of prayers, incantations, or ritual. Millions of Catholics recite a ritual incantation on their rosary beads every day, while the church actively sells (or has sold) "relics," medals, and other items that are thought to possess "magic" powers. The Bible has apparently been used

as a talisman (an object believed to possess supernatural powers or protection) by fervent Protestants, and the cross is viewed as a potent object by many Christians of different denominations. Being "born again," spirit possession, and other acts of ecstasy are regular features of some Protestant sects.

The fact is that there is no such thing as a "primitive" religion, and *all* of the religions of the world make use—perhaps equally—of the tools of the shaman. These tools include liturgy (ritual), songs, incantations (recited prayers or formulas), and direct contact with the spiritual world (visions, ecstasy) in order to bring about changes on the physical plane.

But what about the idea that the shaman believes in "an unseen world of gods, demons, and ancestral spirits"? Many Roman Catholics believe in "an unseen world" of Mother Mary, Father God, Jesus, the Holy Ghost, the devil, many angels and saints (ancestral spirits), plus various demons that can be exorcised. Most Protestants believe in Father God, Jesus, the Holy Ghost, the devil, numerous angels, and a certain number of saints. All of these nonhuman, nonphysical beings would be called "gods" or "lesser gods" if we were being objective, that is, not talking about supposedly monotheistic Christianity.

All modern anthropologists were originally of European descent. Their self-defined mission was to look at "exotic" peoples and to ignore European traditions, by and large. Thus, Christian cults and practices have often escaped being the focus of anthropological theories. Roman Catholic priests and Pentecostal preachers have been spared close study (except for a few off-beat sects such as the rattlesnake handlers of the Appalachians).

Many Native critics and their supporters continue to object to the use of the term *shaman* as applied to indigenous traditional doctors, holy people, herbalists, wise people, vision-seekers, and diagnosticians. Most Native groups have a wide range of individuals who participate, in some way, in the realms of healing and curing, and virtually the entire community participates in the spiritual life—praying, seeking visions, dreaming, helping others, organizing ceremonies, and feeding people at ceremonies. As White Buffalo Woman is reported to have told the Lakota people a thousand years ago, "Every dawn as it comes is a holy event, every day is holy, for the light comes from your father Wakan-Tanka." When seen in this light, the entire world is "magic," all around us, all of the time.

In the view of many historians, "shamanism" is in reality a new European game that should be played by Europeans (or Euro-Americans) without stealing the symbols of indigenous cultures.

— J. D. Forbes

SEE ALSO:
Ceremonies, Exploitation of; New Age Movement; Philosophy, Native.

SUGGESTED READINGS:
Deloria, Vine. *God Is Red.* New York: Dell, 1973.

Gill, Sam D., and Irene F. Sullivan. *Dictionary of Native American Mythology.* New York: Oxford University Press, 1992.

Hirschfelder, Arlene, and Paulette Molin. *Encyclopedia of Native American Religions.* New York: Facts On File, 1992.

Wall, Steve, and Harvey Arden. *Wisdomkeepers: Meetings with Native American Spiritual Elders.* Hillsboro, OR: Beyond Words Publishing, 1990.

SHAWNEE

The Shawnees are an Algonquian-speaking nation that has historically been associated with both the Ohio River Valley and the South. Both the oral traditions of the Shawnees and archaeological evidence, as well as oral traditions of other tribes, credit the Shawnees with a long presence in both regions of the North American continent. The name Shawnee is derived from Algonquian words meaning "south" or "southerner." By the time the United States began encroaching upon Indian lands west of the Appalachians, most of the Shawnees were to be found in the Ohio River Valley. However, they maintained many ties with old neighbors in the South, particularly with several towns of the Muscogee (Creek) Confederation, with which they sought alliances against the westward expansion of the United States in the early nineteenth century. Tecumseh, a Shawnee leader of great vision, and his brother, Tenkswatawa, known as the Prophet, attempted to unite the Eastern Woodlands tribes to counter U.S. expansion, but the attempt failed when Tecumseh was killed in 1813 during the War of 1812, in which he had allied himself with the British.

Most Shawnee bands were removed to the West after 1830. Some, however, eluded removal and remained in the Ohio River Valley, discreetly practicing the Shawnee culture and attempting to blend in with the farming economy of the region. In 1980, a number of these Shawnees, organized as the Shawnee Nation United Remnant Band, gained state recognition of their status as an Indian nation from the state of Ohio. The group numbers about six hundred people. In 1989 they began purchasing tribal land, acquiring 117 acres (46.8 hectares) near Urbana, Ohio, and 63 acres (25.2 hectares) near Chillicothe, Ohio.

The largest group of Shawnees, today numbering about eight thousand, were removed to a reservation of their own in Kansas. They are known as the Loyal Shawnees because of their Union sympathies during the U.S. Civil War. Their loyalty, however, gained them nothing. In 1869, they were forced to move from Kansas and were relocated among the Cherokees in present-day northeastern Oklahoma (then part of the Indian Territory).

Cornstalk, the Shawnee leader who initially resisted the English settlement of Indian lands west of the Appalachians in the 1700s. After bitter fighting, in 1774 Cornstalk signed a treaty with the Earl of Dunmore, then governor of Virginia, in which the Shawnees gave up some of their lands.

known as the Absentee Shawnees, which today number about two thousand, were settled near the Citizen Band Potawatomi Nation near the east-central Oklahoma town of Shawnee, where they gained title to their land by a treaty with the United States in 1872. The nation maintains its own tribal enterprises, health clinics, courts of law, and police force. The largest number of speakers of the Shawnee language belong to the Absentee Shawnees.

The other federally recognized Oklahoma Shawnee tribe is known as the Eastern Shawnees, who are found in Ottawa County, in extreme northeastern Oklahoma. After their removal in 1832 they were associated with the Senecas of that area, but they were separately recognized by a treaty in 1867. They, too, maintain their own tribal economic and governmental enterprises, and their population today stands at more than one thousand.

The largest concentration of Loyal Shawnees is near Whiteoak, Oklahoma. Upon their removal from Kansas, they lost their legal status as a separate nation, and their individual members are today carried on the Cherokee rolls. The Loyal Shawnees maintain their own rolls, however, so that awards for judgments against the federal government can be disbursed fairly among tribal members and their descendants. Between 1929 and 1984, they won four court cases against the United States that resulted in monetary judgments.

Two other Shawnee bands are federally recognized Indian nations in Oklahoma. Both of them organized in the late 1930s under the Oklahoma Indian Welfare Act of 1936. The largest of the two,

SEE ALSO:
Civil War, U.S., Indians in the; Oklahoma; Removal Act, Indian; Tecumseh; Tippecanoe, Battle of.

SHAWNEE PROPHET (TENSKWATAWA)

SEE Tecumseh.

SHENANDOAH, JOANNE
(c. 1960–)

Oneida musician Joanne Shenandoah became a major presence in Native American folk music late in the twentieth century, fusing traditional songs with western music and other styles. In 1993, she was recognized by the First Americans in the Arts Foundation as its Musician of the Year.

Shenandoah is the daughter of Maisie Shenandoah, a clan mother, and Clifford Shenandoah, an Onondaga chief and jazz guitarist. Clifford Shenandoah was one of a line of Oneida chiefs reaching back to Skenandoah, who organized the Oneidas to feed General George Washington's Continental Army during a bitter winter at Valley Forge, Pennsylvania.

Shenandoah married Mohawk editor and activist Doug George and, with him, formed Round Dance Productions of Oneida, New York. Shenandoah and George have produced films, books, and other media that combine entertainment with themes emphasizing Native American rights and history.

From her earliest years, Shenandoah was urged to study music and to make use of her voice. Though she made a living as an architectural designer for fourteen years, her rediscovery of her people's stories and songs prompted Shenandoah to begin a singing career.

Shenandoah's enchanting voice has been likened to "a Native American trance." By the mid-1990s, she had released five collections of songs in the United States, as well as one single ("Nature Dance") in Germany and a collection of dance music in Spain. Shenandoah opened the 1994 concert at Woodstock before an audience of about 250,000 people. She also contributed to a record album issued in defense of Leonard Peltier (convicted, under what many feel to have been questionable circumstances, of murdering two FBI agents in a shootout on the Pine Ridge Reservation in South Dakota) and helped organize a concert of Native American women singers at the White House.

Shenandoah's music was featured on the Canadian Broadcasting Corporation's documentary "The War Against the Indian" and several local and national PBS documentaries in the United States. She had a role in the musical score of the commercial television series *Northern Exposure* and sang a song about the repatriation of Native American remains that was played four times during one segment of Cable News Network's *Larry King Live*. "Hopefully," Shenandoah said after the song was

Joanne Shenandoah, Oneida singer and songwriter, at work in her studio at her home in Oneida, New York.

played on the talk show, "my listeners, Indian or not, can begin to see the human side of Indian problems."

SEE ALSO:
Oneida; Peltier, Leonard; Pine Ridge Reservation, Conflict at; Reburial and Repatriation of Human Remains and Sacred Objects; Skenandoah.

SHIELD DANCE

The Shield Dance allows warriors to express themselves using a highly decorated shield made of buffalo skin and often a spear. Although the dance was primarily a Plains Indian tradition, many intertribal groups incorporate characteristics of their own culture into versions of the dance today. For example, the Pueblos of New Mexico have infused Pueblo-style dress into the Shield Dance. Still, the

A Shield Dancer at an event in the Santa Fe Indian Market. Although the roots of the Shield Dance lie primarily with Plains Indians groups, it has been adopted—and adapted—by various Native communities, including many in New Mexico.

A young Comanche Shield Dancer performs at the San Juan Pueblo Feast Day in New Mexico.

basic intent of the dance has survived throughout North America, and although various versions of the Shield Dance have been popularized, a few standard songs still continue its basic themes.

The Shield Dance usually consists of two dancers dressed in magnificent outfits carrying a spear and shield. The dancer's dress or outfit includes some type of headdress, either a war bonnet or traditional war dancer's roach (a strip of animal hair or fur worn tied securely across the top of the head).

The shield was originally made from the shoulder hide of the buffalo. As many as four or five layers of thick tough buffalo hide could be stretched over a circular wooden frame. The shield was so durable and heavy that a flying object like an arrow, tomahawk, spear, or rock could not penetrate it. Warriors developed great skill in the use of their shields, mainly to protect themselves. They danced to display their technique of shielding themselves from objects thrown at them and demonstrated their cunning rhythm. Today, many shields comprise

cardboard, thin masonite, or plywood decorated with tribal designs and feathers. Attached to the back side of the shield are straps and tie strings. These help the dancers hold their shields firmly so they never drop to the ground. Some dancers sew heavy cloth covers for the face of the shield. Spears were made from any straight and sharp wooden stick.

The dance begins by having the dancers face each other and go through the motions of two fighting warriors. The dancers taunt each other before moving into their more rigorous body movements, always keeping in rhythm with the songs being sung and the beat of the drum in the background. The rhythm of the dance goes both fast and slow: As the songs and drumbeats speed up, so do the dancers. The dance slows to give the dancers an opportunity to rest; then the drummers gradually pick up the beat.

During the Shield Dance, dancers run toward each other, then retreat to recover and rest. Still dancing in place, both warriors charge one another again, fiercely darting and moving their weapons as if to throw them. The dancers bend forward from their hips and move their shields and spears back and forth in front of their bodies. While performing these fluid movements, the dancers eye one another suspiciously. While in full movement, each dancer wards off his opponent's spears with his shield in skillful rhythms accompanying the drum. Following their combative movements, the dancers proudly wave their weapons slowly in the air as they perform a fast war-dance beat. This stage of the Shield Dance signifies that the dancer's skill has brought victory to the warrior.

The dancers move in a figure-eight configuration throughout the dance. The warriors constantly shout war cries and use various smooth movements to intimidate their opponents. The final song is a fast war-dance song that signifies a victory for both dancers. Both dancers end the dance by facing in the same direction.

The singers never cease beating the drum throughout the Shield Dance performance. After the dancers complete their final routines, the drumbeats stop, thereby concluding the Shield Dance.

SEE ALSO:

Dance, American Indian; Drums.

SHOSHONE

The term *Shoshone* (also spelled *Shoshoni*) is applied to three groups of indigenous peoples who inhabited the Great Basin area of North America. At the time of European contact, the Northern Shoshones occupied eastern Idaho, northern Utah, western Montana, and eastern Oregon. The Eastern (or Wind River) Shoshones were located in western Wyoming. The Comanches were an offshoot of this group— breaking away and moving southeast to Texas after acquiring horses in the seventeenth century. The Western Shoshones roamed an area that included central and north Nevada, western Idaho, northwestern Utah, and the Panamint and Death Valleys of California. The Shoshone language belongs to the Numic group of the Uto-Aztecan language family.

The Shoshones took advantage of the specific natural resources available to each group; this was reflected in their political, economic, and social development. The Western Shoshones inhabited a barren desolate landscape with very few resources; they were the least politically and economically developed of the groups. They lived in small bands and came together as a larger group perhaps only once a year.

An undated photograph from the 1800s of a Shoshone, named Rabbit Tail, who worked as a member of a Euro-American scouting company. Many Shoshone groups fell into a wide variety of alliances and conflicts with the United States government, and non-Indian settlers.

Constantly on the move to wherever resources were available, the Western Shoshones traveled primarily on foot (the word *Shoshono* means "walking"), and their beast of burden was the dog. Even though horses were introduced to the Great Basin in the seventeenth century, the Western Shoshones did not adapt to their use because their environment would not support the grazing of horses.

The Western Shoshones subsisted primarily by eating seeds and plants. They supplemented their plant diet by hunting and fishing where possible. The spiritual and social life of the Western Shoshones matched the simplicity of their lifestyle. They worshiped a principle deity, Apo, the sun, and what ceremonies they practiced were centered on a round dance. This basic description of the Western Shoshones applies to their relatives to the north and east prior to contact with Great Plains culture and their introduction to the horse.

The Northern Shoshones fall somewhere in between the Eastern and Western Shoshones in terms of political, economic, and social development. While there was no single tribe of Northern Shoshones, they did tend to gather in larger villages and for longer periods of time than the Western Shoshones. The more eastern of the Northern Shoshones, including the Lemhis, acquired the buffalo-hunting and horse culture of the Plains Indians, at least for part of the year, but the tribes to the southwest used horses sparingly and were much more closely related to the Western Shoshones. What makes them unique is their adaptation to the Plateau culture to their north and its dependence on salmon and other fish. Their fishing activities were centered on the Snake River and its tributaries. These tribes also used the bulb of the camas lily as a primary source of food because it could be dried and stored

A contemporary Shoshone jingle dancer performing at a 1995 powwow in Idaho.

for use in wintertime. Politically, the Northern Shoshones were more complex as well; the larger villages had chiefs who directed hunting and fishing activities and made alliances with other tribes, particularly when they crossed over onto the Plains to hunt buffalo. Their religion also showed influence of the Plateau culture to the north and the Plains to the east. In particular, there was evidence of the Sun Dance from the Plains culture.

The Eastern Shoshones were the most politically, socially, and economically developed of the Shoshone groups. Earlier in Shoshone history, they

Bedecked in regalia that includes symbols adopted from the U.S. flag, a Shoshone elder participates in the Grand Entry of a tribal powwow.

had penetrated beyond the Great Basin and onto the Great Plains and as far north as Canada. They were later forced back into the Great Basin under pressure from Blackfeet, Sioux, and Cheyennes—themselves forced westward by settlers. But the Shoshones brought back with them a lifestyle more reminiscent of Natives of the Plains, in particular, a culture dominated by big-game hunting, especially the buffalo, and warfare. Because buffalo hunting was more efficient in large groups, the Shoshones would gather from spring until fall for the hunt. At this time, they would generally gather under a single chief, such as the famous Washakie, for buffalo hunting and waging war to preserve hunting grounds. This process became easier with the introduction of the horse in the seventeenth century. During the winter months, they would break into smaller kinship groups and camp in sheltered valleys that could support small herds of horses. These Shoshones were also known to participate in the intertribal rendezvous at Fort Bridger,

Wyoming, where they traded goods with other tribes and with European-American traders. Religion for the Eastern Shoshones was based on the elaborate rituals of the Sun Dance.

European contact with the Shoshones began in the early nineteenth century. At that time, contact was limited to explorers, fur trappers, and traders. European intrusion and settlement increased by midcentury, influenced by the discovery of gold in California and Nevada, the opening of the Oregon Trail, and permanent settlement in the Great Basin by the Mormons. The reaction to this incursion by the Shoshones was varied. The Eastern Shoshones, under the influence of Chief Washakie, allied themselves with the non-Indians in warfare against the Cheyenne and Sioux. They were rewarded with the granting of a huge reservation centered in the Wind River Valley, Wyoming—a reservation that has been dramatically reduced in size over the years as a result of the vagaries of U.S. Indian policy.

The Northern Shoshones resisted the European invasion but were defeated at the Battle of Bear River in 1863, in what has been called the Bannock Wars. They were put on several reservations, including the Fort Hall Reservation in Idaho and the Duck Valley Reservation along the Nevada-Oregon border. The Western Shoshones put up resistance as well, but, in accordance with treaties signed in 1863, they gave up their way of life to reside on reservations.

Reservation life for the Shoshones has been difficult. The first years were characterized by a sharp decline in population, and even though recent times have seen population levels increase to near pre-reservation levels, the Shoshones continue to struggle with unemployment, alcoholism, and a general lack of opportunity.

They have also been involved in an ongoing legal struggle with both the federal and state governments to define and retain their rights. The Western Shoshones have long argued that the treaty of 1863 never gave away their land and have taken that issue all the way to the U.S. Supreme Court. They have also been in a dispute with the Bureau of Land Management over grazing rights in Nevada. Plus, the Eastern Shoshones have been fighting for water rights in Wyoming, and there has been an ongoing dispute with the federal government over the disposal of nuclear waste on their lands. The introduction of the gaming industry on some reservation land has provided the potential of economic security for some Shoshone tribes.

— T. Marshall

SEE ALSO:

Blackfeet; Bureau of Land Management; Cheyenne; Gold Rush; Horses; Mormons; Oregon Trail; Sacajawea; Siouan Nations.

SUGGESTED READINGS:

Corless, Hank. *The Weiser Indians: Shoshoni Peacemakers.* Salt Lake City: University of Utah Press, 1990.

Crum, Steven J. *The Road on Which We Came—Poũ Pentun Tammen Kimmappeh: A History of the Western Shoshoni.* Salt Lake City: University of Utah Press, 1994.

Madsen, Brigham D. *The Shoshoni Frontier and the Bear River Massacre.* Salt Lake City: University of Utah Press, 1985.

Trenholm, Virginia Cole, and Maurice Carley. *The Shoshonis.* Norman: University of Oklahoma Press, 1964.

Voget, Fred W. *The Shoshoni-Crow Sun Dance.* Norman: University of Oklahoma Press, 1984.

SIGN LANGUAGE, NATIVE

Long before Europeans arrived in North America, Native Americans throughout the continent were using sign language to conduct a thriving trade in furs, fish, corn, copper, and many other goods. Because Native people spoke approximately six hundred dialects in many different languages, they often communicated with each other in signs they all knew. Although anthropologists are not sure where in North America sign language first origi-

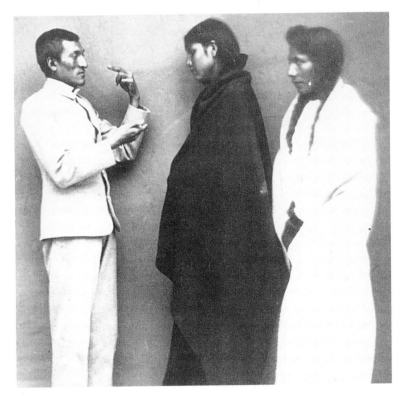

In this 1878 photo, a Cheyenne resident of the Hampton Institute in Virginia uses the sign language of the Plains Indians cultures to welcome two newcomers from the Dakota Territory. Hampton was a school that brought together Indian students from a wide range of cultures.

In this undated photo, a young Pequot man converses with his mother in sign language at their home in Connecticut.

ples had trouble communicating with one another. These Europeans often found Indian sign language an easier way to get information or negotiate trade than trying to learn the Native languages or forcing the people they encountered to learn English, Spanish, or Dutch. (When Lewis and Clark met the Flathead Indians in 1805, for example, their questions had to be interpreted through six languages before the Flatheads understood them.) Colonizers from Columbus to Coronado relied at least in part on sign language to communicate with the people they encountered. Some, like W. P. Clark (of the exploring team Lewis and Clark), wrote what were essentially sign "dictionaries" that tried precisely to describe the appropriate hand signs Native Americans had developed for hundreds of words and concepts.

Sign language is by no means a primitive form of communication that was used simply for trading or giving directions. It is a highly complex language that has been used for hundreds of years to express customs and cultural traditions, to pass on myths and legends, and to articulate abstract spiritual concepts. It is a language with rules of grammar covering past, present, and future tenses, precise adjectives and adverbs, colorful metaphors, and idiomatic expressions. Signing gestures are made in fluid, sweeping gestures, making conversations graceful and elegant to watch.

nated, they agree that it became most highly developed by American Indian cultures of the Western Plains such as the Crow, Cheyenne, Plains Ojibwe (Plains Chippewa), Blackfeet, and Pawnee. While some of the gestures differed slightly from culture to culture, they were usually alike enough to be understood by Indians from Canada to Mexico.

Early European explorers and settlers in North America had difficulty communicating with Native cultures for the same reasons that indigenous peo-

Here are some simple examples of signing. For "child," hold the right hand, compressed into a fist, upward at the right side and then lower the hand to the height of the child. "Tired" is expressed by holding the hands, backs up, several inches apart well in front of the body, with only the index fingers extended and the other fingers slightly curled; lower the hands slightly and draw them slightly toward the body. To talk about "yesterday," bring extended hands, backs up, up in front of the body with the fingers pointing to the front, then sweep the right hand upward and to the right in a curve, bringing it down to the same height as the left hand while at the same time turning the back of the hand down.

Signals are another form of sign language that were used to communicate over large distances or as a secret code during battle. Signals could be made by riding or dismounting a pony a certain way to indicate that an enemy was nearby or by holding or folding a blanket a certain way to indicate a desire to negotiate a peace (or to refuse to surrender). Mirrors and smoke signals (puffs of smoke created by covering and uncovering a fire with a blanket) were employed to warn people at a distance of an approaching enemy or of the sighting of a buffalo herd.

Today, many Native American cultures are expressing a renewed interest in the language of signing as a rich part of their cultural heritage.

SILKO, LESLIE MARMON (1948–)

Leslie Marmon Silko was born in Albuquerque, New Mexico. Her heritage is part Laguna, and she grew up at Laguna Pueblo.

After high school, Silko graduated from the University of New Mexico and then spent more than a year studying in the American Indian Law Program before deciding to become a writer.

Leslie M. Silko has written several novels and books of poetry, most of which draws upon her ancestors' heritage. Her stories and poems have appeared in many magazines and collections, but she is best known for her two novels, *Ceremony* and *Almanac of the Dead*. For her achievement in writing, she has been recognized by a National Endowment for the Arts Writing Fellowship and has earned a five-year MacArthur Foundation Grant. She has also been involved in filmmaking about the Laguna people and has taught at the University of New Mexico and the University of Arizona.

Silko has two children and lives in Tucson, Arizona.

SILVERHEELS, JAY (c. 1919-1980)

Born on the Six Nations Reserve in Ontario, Canada, as Harold J. Smith, actor Jay Silverheels became most well known for his television role as Tonto in the popular 1950s television series *The Lone Ranger*. The year of his birth is most often given as 1919 or 1920, although some sources list him as having been born in 1918, and at least one gives the date of his birth as 1912.

Silverheels was raised as a traditional Mohawk and educated on the Six Nations Reserve. He emigrated to the United States in 1933 and first visited Hollywood that same year as a member of a touring professional lacrosse team. He later returned as a professional boxer and in 1938 qualified as a Golden Gloves contender. Actor and comedian Joe E. Brown encouraged Silverheels to consider acting, and the professional athlete and movie extra got his first significant role playing an Indian prince in *The Captain from Castille* (1947), starring Tyrone Power. During the 1950s, Silverheels played the Apache chief Geronimo in three different films. One of them, *Broken Arrow* (1950), is the first film credited with portraying Native Americans sympathetically.

Although Jay Silverheels had thirty-nine film credits to his name, he is most famous for playing Tonto, the Indian sidekick of the Lone Ranger in the long-running television series of the same name. Silverheels acted in all 221 episodes of the series, which ran from 1949 through 1957 and continued in syndicated reruns. (The character of the Lone Ranger, incidentally, which came to be most closely identified with actor Clayton Moore, was also briefly played by John Hart in the 1950s.) While the character Tonto became a stereotyped "faithful Indian companion," Silverheels is also remembered as bringing dignity and wisdom to his work as an actor.

Jay Silverheels, dressed for his role as Tonto, companion to the Lone Ranger, visits a young cancer patient at a rodeo in New York City in 1951. Silverheels was admired both for his professionalism as an actor and for his devotion to humanitarian causes.

Silverheels continued to play Tonto in two major *Lone Ranger* movies, both of them featuring Clayton Moore in his familiar role as the Lone Ranger. *The Legend of the Lone Ranger* (1953) traces the story of the Lone Ranger's origins to an ambush and massacre of a group of Texas Rangers by the vicious Cavendish gang; one of the Texas Rangers, left for dead, is found and nursed back to physical health by Tonto, who forms an alliance based on the surviving ranger's sense of justice and thirst for revenge. *The Lone Ranger and the Lost City of Gold* (1958), the second Lone Ranger movie, features an interesting twist on the plot of a typical movie Western involving Indians and whites in battle: The Lone Ranger and Tonto come to the aid of Indians who are being attacked by marauding white "bad guys" for their treasure.

The popularity of the TV series gave rise to a huge body of images associated with the show. These include products (masks, silver bullets, models of the horses Silver and Scout), expressions ("Hi-yo Silver, away"; "Who was that masked man?"; "Come back with us to those thrilling days of yesteryear . . ."), music (the William Tell Overture as the show's theme), and even jokes that survive to this day. Many of the jokes center on the subservient role that Tonto played to his "Kemosabe" (pronounced KEE-mo-SAH-bee), the name he called the Lone Ranger, and on the broken English that Indians supposedly spoke back in those "days of yesteryear." The relationship between the characters popularized by Silverheels and Moore has become for many a symbol of relations between Indians and non-Indians and for the portrayal of Indians in American Westerns. A 1994 collection of short fiction by Sherman Alexie (Spokane-Coeur d'Alene), for example, is named *The Lone Ranger and Tonto Fistfight in Heaven,* after one of its stories.

Most Lone-Ranger-and-Tonto jokes actually hinge on sympathy for Tonto as an abused underdog, the Indian who justifiably harbors a contemptuous resentment against and sense of superiority over the white man who uses Native Americans' "people" skills, loyalty, and command of the terrain, and then takes all the credit when everything turns out okay. In one popular joke, for example, the Lone Ranger and Tonto are riding through a gully, when they notice a group of "hostile" Indians gathered on the ridge above them. "What do we do now, Tonto?" asks the Lone Ranger of his faithful Indian companion. Tonto glances at the Indians and then at the Lone Ranger and replies, " What you mean 'we,' Paleface?"

A cartoon in Gary Larson's *Far Side* series depicts an older man sitting in a chair reading an *"Indian Dictionary,"* a black mask hanging on a hook behind him. The caption beneath the cartoon reads, "The Lone Ranger, long since retired, makes an unpleasant discovery." In the cartoon, the retired Masked Man says to himself as he reads his dictionary, "Oh, here it is. . . . 'Kemosabe. Apache expression for a horse's rear end.' What the hey? . . ."

Silverheel's life was thus unavoidably bound up in his role as the Indian companion of a Texas Ranger (probably no friend of Native people in his campaigns against them in nineteenth-century Texas). And yet, not only did he bring dignity to his roles on the screen, but he also distinguished himself among his colleagues and the public as an actor, a humanitarian, and a human being. In 1963, Silverheels founded the Indian Actors Workshop in Hollywood as a way of assisting aspiring Native American actors. Around this same time, he also worked with various public service projects focusing on substance abuse and the elderly. He also was a family man. Married in 1946 to Mary Di Roma, who was an Italian-American, they had four children: Marilyn, Pamela, Karen, and Jay Anthony.

Once the popularity of movie Westerns waned in the 1960s and 1970s, Silverheels, who was heavily identified with the role of Tonto, found it increasingly difficult to find work. Nonetheless, he continued to appear in films with Western themes, such as *True Grit* (1969) and *The Man Who Loved Cat Dancing* (1973). In 1974, he obtained a harness racing license and participated in the world of professional horse racing from 1974 to 1977. In August 1979, Silverheels became the first Native actor to have a star set in Hollywood's Walk of Fame.

Jay Silverheels died in Woodland Hills, California, at the Motion Picture and Television Country House on March 5, 1980, from complications arising from pneumonia.

— M. J. Sachner / M. A. Stout

SEE ALSO:

Entertainment and the Performing Arts; Hollywood, Indians, and Indian Images; Texas Rangers.

SUGGESTED READINGS:

Calder, Jenni. *There Must Be a Lone Ranger*. New York: Taplinger Publishing Company, 1974.

Friar, Natalie, and Ralph Friar. *The Only Good Indian: The Hollywood Gospel*. New York: Drama Book Specialist/Publishers, 1972.

French, Philip. *Westerns*. New York: Oxford University Press, 1977.

Hirschfelder, Arlene B. *American Indian Stereotypes in the World of Children*. Metuchen, NJ: The Scarecrow Press, Inc., 1982.

O'Connor, John E. *The Hollywood Indian: Stereotypes of Native Americans in Film*. Trenton, NJ: New Jersey State Museum, 1980.

SILVERSMITHING, NAVAJO

Navajo jewelry, especially work done in silver and turquoise, is internationally famous. Navajo silversmithing dates from the arrival of a Mexican silversmith at Fort Defiance, Arizona, in 1853. 'Atsidi Sani learned the craft from him and taught it to others. By 1867, several Navajos were working with silver.

While interned by the U.S. Army at Bosque Redondo in eastern New Mexico as prisoners of war, Navajos who had already learned silversmithing found another application for their talents. Their food rations at Bosque Redondo were administered by a method that involved issuing the Navajos stamped pieces of metal as ration coupons. The Navajos soon made their own metal dies and created their own counterfeit stamps, thereby greatly increasing the amount of food they received from the army.

A Navajo silversmith poses with his work in a photo taken around 1880.

By 1880, Navajos had begun to combine turquoise with their designs, producing a jewelry that has become known as distinctly Navajo. At the famous Hubbell Trading Post, traders were quick to see the commercial prospects for Navajo jewelry. In the late ninteenth century, Hubbell brought in more Mexican silversmiths to teach the craft to even more Navajos. Mexican and U.S. silver coins, such as silver dollars, were used for raw material. By the turn of the century, the Fred Harvey Company asked Navajo silversmiths to make lighter pieces for the tourist trade and guaranteed them a sales outlet. Today, silversmithing is a craft practiced by many Navajos.

SEE ALSO:
Bosque Redondo; Jewelry, Native; Navajo; Navajo Reservation.

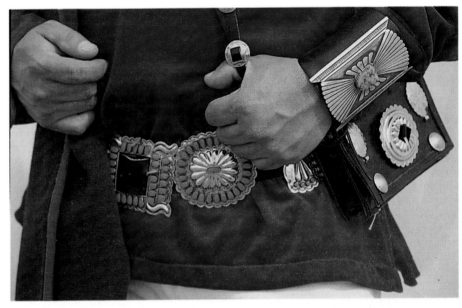

A member of a Navajo dance group displays a variety of items featuring designs in silver. The combination of silver and turquoise creates a distinctly Native American look that is recognized worldwide.

SINAGUA

The Sinagua people were one of the most remarkable and adaptive cultures of the Southwest, whose best-known cultural period roughly parallels that of their northern neighbors, the Anasazi (1000–1300 C.E.). But unlike the widespread Anasazi, Sinagua culture encompassed only a small area in the San Francisco Mountains near present-day Flagstaff, Arizona.

The Sinaguas are credited with discovering a solution to the most pressing problem of the Southwest—lack of sufficient water, especially for cultivating crops. Their mountainous environment provided only enough precipitation for cultivation at elevations above 7,000 feet (2,123 meters), but at those elevations, the growing season was short. The Sinaguas discovered that the residue of volcanic eruptions in the area, cinder and ash, could be used as a mulch that conserved moisture, as well as providing nutrients for the crops. It also allowed them to cultivate land at lower elevations where rainfall was sparse but the growing season was long.

The Sinaguas were provided with an unexpected sudden bounty during the winter of 1064 to 1065 with the spectacular birth of a new volcano, Sunset Crater. It belched forth a rain of cinder and ash that left the Sinaguas in the midst of an 800-square-mile (2,080-square-kilometer) area of new agricultural lands.

This sudden enrichment set off a cultural boom that lasted for a century and a half and is distinguished for reasons other than the rapid increase in population and economic activity. Neighboring Indian civilizations learned about the rich potential of these new agricultural lands, and soon farmers from all directions began arriving. From the east came the Mogollon, from the north the Anasazi, from the south the Hohokam, and from the west the Cohonino. Instead of creating friction, these groups mingled and shared their knowledge with one another. Ideas regarding building techniques, recreation, religion, and arts and crafts passed back and forth. The Sinaguas proved especially adaptable to new ideas. They admired Anasazi skill and techniques in the architectural use of masonry and adopted those practices for their own. They also adopted Hohokam irrigation techniques, as well as their ritual ball court games and some of

Montezuma Castle National Monument, Arizona, so named because of the mistaken belief that the Aztec leader Moctezuma (whose name is often spelled Montezuma in English) had come here, is a Sinagua landmark.

their crafts. Within a short period of time, the Sinaguas had transformed into a new people.

The center of this cultural mingling is now preserved as Wapatki National Monument, north of Flagstaff and near the west bank of the Little Colorado River. Other Sinagua sites, some of which include spectacular cliff dwellings, are Walnut Canyon National Monument, Tuzigoot National Monument, and Montezuma Castle National Monument.

Eventually, a severe, prolonged drought reduced the amount of available moisture to a point where the ash farming method could no longer be practiced, and Sinagua sites, like those of the Anasazi, were abandoned. No one knows what happened to the Sinagua people. But some theorists have speculated that they may have migrated to the Hopi mesas and become the Hopi people of today, who have a deep reverence for the San Francisco Mountains, home of their kachina spirits.

SEE ALSO:
Anasazi; Hohokam; Mogollon.

SINGING

Throughout American Indian history, many ceremonial songs arose from Native American tribes as they experienced life and death, the excitement of war, and the joys of peace. Each song had a purpose and was carefully formulated; each one was created to be studied and remembered. Tribes preserved historical events and special individual moments through their song rituals.

Within many traditional Native rituals, music, like sound itself, is treated as one of the ancient natural forces from the creative power of the Great Mystery. Within these traditions, sounds, including music, may be said to actually exist in space, which is also a part of nature, and music is looked upon as the sound of the natural world. According to this view, Indian singing is a fusion of humans and nature. Even today, the entire sound of Indian music, with its movement and rhythmical reality, is rooted in these traditions. Singing comes from the heart, interweaving the spiritual realm with the everyday world and broadening the Native peoples in many special ways. Most Indian singing is a result of close communion with nature, and many singers feel that their inspiration comes from songs heard only in a vision or dream. This event or process is natural (based on intuition and spiritual feelings), instead of rational (based on reasoning and the mind).

Most traditional Indian beliefs hold that unseen spirits were often stirred by the songs—that offensive songs brought bad fortune, while pleasing songs invoked the unseen spirits of nature and brought aid from the appropriate spirits. Traditionally, Native people had songs for everything in nature—victories, the four winds, bubbling springs, painted clouds, the rainbow—because songs brought them into friendly harmony with all created images and things.

Singing is also part of the oral tradition, and because Indian singing does not traditionally have any schematic musical notation, it generally cannot be written down. The oral folk memory must preserve it. Traditionally, Indian people learned songs by rote, listening to singers who themselves had remarkable memories. To this day, many singers are able to learn a new song by hearing it sung only a few times, even if it is from a different tribe.

This oral tribal music is performed as part of the larger cultural activity usually referred to as a dance. Without song, there can be no dance, and therefore, it is impossible to separate song from dance. In different tribes and regions, many songs vary according to the gender of the dancers, as well as according to the patterns, rhythm, and steps of the songs. To help the beginner learn the dances, many of the dances' more complicated variations are purposely omitted, with only the simpler and more popular patterns being presented. In some explanations of the dances, important variations are merely mentioned.

Most Indian songs are chants accompanied by beating drums or shaking rattles. The rhythm pat-

A group of young men sing and play traditional drum songs at the Dene community of Trout Lake in the Northwest Territories, Canada.

An Inuit elder in Qaanaaq, Greenland, accompanies himself on a traditional drum, hitting only the rim.

terns are simple and consist of steady beats on the drum. Some more complicated rhythm patterns involve drumrolls, rests, and short and long beats. To simplify the presentation of the rhythm patterns, standard musical notes, terms, and symbols are used.

Songs are, in some cases, continuations of mythological cycles or stories, recitations of events that take place in a visionary or superhistorical world; in other cases, songs are invocations of particular helping spirits or of the Great Spirit. But in any event, these songs are often an expression of gratitude for what has been given us human beings. Generally simple on the surface, songs or chants are part of a ritual cycle of great complexity, with symbols that reveal people as completely interlinked with nature, the sky, and the spirits.

In addition to their religious meanings, songs may also contain tribal words that carry special meanings. Tribal words—words that are of particular significance to a particular tribe—occur in word songs, which usually tell a story about a significant event. Tribal words may relate to specific visions, deeds, births, or any other milestones in the life of a warrior of a certain tribe.

Indian singing may sound strange to ears unaccustomed to Indian music. Songs are accompanied by drums and wind instruments, and some singers sing high-pitched notes, while other tribal groups sing in voices that carry low, mellow tones.

Some singers have no system of notation, only symbols on the drum or some other object to remind them of certain songs. These songs are passed on, with their interpretations, from one generation to another. Students of Indian music have found that Indian songs can be transcribed in musical notation, but not accurately. Indian singing can also be analyzed as to key and mode as in Western music, although it is a challenging task.

Many tribes designate a lead singer to begin most or all of their tribal ceremonial songs. Today's powwow singing may involve many lead singers at the drum at the same time. For singers to communicate while singing, sign language is used to signify various treatment of the songs. While beating the drum with a drumstick in one hand, the singer will make signs with his opposite hand, giving instructions to the other singers. This interchange of movement flows smoothly throughout long hours of group singing.

Although singing on the big drum is traditionally designated for the men, women are also accomplished singers. Many women start creating songs while their babies are still unborn with the rhythm of the drum providing the baby with its first ritual heartbeat. Women sing different versions of their lullaby songs or chants, all of which are soft and pleasing to the ear. The woman's voice is one of the first common elements of sound in an infant's early life. Other singers may be both adult women and young women, as well as elders and children who sing children's songs. For these singers—people of all ages and of any gender—Indian singing means tradition, movement, and inspiration.

— C. Pewewardy

SEE ALSO:

Dance, American Indian; Drums; Music and Musical Instruments; Sign Language, Native.

SUGGESTED READINGS:

Braine, Susan. *Drumbeat Heartbeat: A Celebration of the Powwow*. Minneapolis: Lerner Publications Company, 1995.

Heth, Charlotte, ed. *Native American Dance: Ceremonies and Social Traditions*. Washington, DC: National Museum of the American Indian with Starwood Publishing, Inc., 1992.

SIOUAN LANGUAGES

Despite efforts by early European colonists and the government of the United States to eradicate American Indian languages, especially through the institution of Indian boarding schools, most Indian languages live on. About one-third of all Native people north of Mexico still speak their native languages, which fall into groups such as these: Algonquian, Athabascan, Caddoan, Eskimo-Aleut, Iroquoian, Keresan, Muskogean, Penutian, Salishan, Siouan, Tanoan, Uto-Aztecan, and Zuni. The Navajo, Iroquois (people of the Mohawk, Oneida, Onondaga, Seneca, and Tuscarora Nations), Inuit, Papagos-Pima, Apache, and Sioux

This photographic portrait, taken by famed photographer Edward S. Curtis early in the twentieth century, is of a Sioux woman and her child.

of past United States government efforts to eradicate members of the tribes, their languages, or both.

Under the phylum Macro-Siouan, the Siouan Family consists of the languages spoken by the Sioux (Dakota), Hidatsa-Crow, Assiniboine, Omaha, Ponca, Osage, Kansa, Quapaw, Iowa, Oto, Missouri, Winnebago, Mandan, Kaw, and Catawba peoples. With the exception of the Catawbas, who lived in the Southeast in the area of present-day North Carolina and Kentucky, these are the people of the Great Plains who made their homes in the midsection of the present-day United States and Canada. (Red Thunder Cloud, the last known living speaker of the Catawba language, died in Worcester, Massachusetts, in January 1996.)

The Siouan-speaking Dakota and the Hidatsa-Crow arrived in present-day Minnesota, Wisconsin, and Manitoba (Canada) sometime prior to the fourteenth century. In the seventeenth century, the Hidatsa-Crow were forced to flee to the edge of the Great Plains just beyond the Missouri River by armed Crees and Ojibwes (Chippewas). The Crow eventually settled along the Yellowstone River.

The Assiniboine (an element of the Sioux) are known as "those who cook with stone." Their original territory was around the Great Lakes. The Eastern Assiniboine are now in Montana on the Fort Belknap and Fort Peck Reservations, and the so-called Stoneys are in Saskatchewan and Alberta in Canada. The tribe's language, which is part of the Dakota dialect complex, is one of the Siouan languages spoken in historical times on the Plains. There are some differences between the dialect spoken by Assiniboines at Fort Peck and the dialect spoken at Fort Belknap. At one time in the not-so-distant past, the speakers of the native Assiniboine language numbered fewer than fifty.

have the highest number of members still retaining their native tongue. Some groups, such as the Cherokee, Choctaw, Creek, Lummi, Mohawk, Muckleshoot, Navajo, and Sioux, have created dictionaries and school programs in their native tongues.

The various elements of the Sioux, with their high visibility and historic involvement in numerous conflicts between the U.S. government and Native people, are among the most representative and compelling examples of a people who have kept their language and culture alive. Today, the numbers of people speaking various languages within the Siouan Family vary according to many factors, including present size of tribe and the results

A group of Oglala Sioux gather at an altar in this historic Edward S. Curtis photograph. Curtis was not a Native photographer, but he made a sincere effort to capture the authenticity of Indian life in America, even if it meant asking his subjects to position themselves in ways that accurately represented their customs and actions.

Today, with tribal leaders working to teach the language to both adults and children, it is used in public ceremonies and has become an important form of ethnic identity for the Assiniboines.

The Omaha, Ponca, Osage, Kansa, and Quapaw tribes lived east of the lower Ohio River Valley in Indiana and Kentucky prior to the seventeenth century. These tribes speak the languages of the Dhegiha Siouan group.

At some point after the Omahas, Poncas, and Quapaws left their homelands in the east, the Omahas and Poncas became separated from the Quapaws. At a crossing on the Ohio River in southern Indiana, the Omahas and Poncas followed the Des Moines River to its headwaters in what is now northwestern Iowa. The Omahas settled on the Missouri River in the 1770s near the present-day town of Homer, Nebraska. The Poncas made their home near the present-day town of Niobrara, Nebraska. The Quapaws continued south and settled in present-day Arkansas. Today, only a very few members of these tribes speak their native language.

The Iowas are made up of two distinct groups: the Southern Iowas in Oklahoma and the Northern Iowas in Kansas and Nebraska. In the 1870s, after the U.S. Civil War, the Southern Iowas moved into Indian Territory (now Oklahoma) and continued to live in their traditional way. The Northern Iowas moved onto lands along the Kansas–Nebraska border near the Missouri River. The language of the Iowa belongs to the Chiwere group of Siouan languages, along with Oto and Missouri. These languages are closely related to Winnebago. (In the sixteenth century, the Oto made their home in present-day Iowa; the Missouri in Missouri and Illinois; and the Winnebago around the Great Lakes.) It is not known how many Iowa members still speak the native language.

The Siouan-speaking Mandans settled along Plains rivers beginning in the thirteenth century. By the sixteenth century, they mainly occupied present-day South Dakota. According to some counts, only six people spoke the Mandan language in 1990.
— B. J. Behm

SIOUAN NATIONS

The Sioux are a confederation of North American Plains peoples speaking the Siouan language. The three main divisions of the Sioux are known as Dakota (Santee), Nakota (Yankton), and Lakota (Teton). The Dakota, or Eastern Sioux, consist of the Mdewakanton, Wahpeton, Wahpekute, and Sisseton tribes. The Nakota (Middle Sioux) include the Yankton and Yanktonai tribes; and the Lakota, or Western Sioux, comprise seven major tribes: Sihasapa (Blackfeet), Brulé, Oglala, Itazipcho (Sans Arc), Hunkpapa, Miniconjou, and Oohenonpa (Two Kettle).

Historically, the Eastern Sioux (Dakota) lived in the Lake Superior area, hunting, gathering, and fishing in a semisedentary Woodlands economy. Hostilities with the Ojibwes (Chippewas) gradually pushed them into Minnesota, and the Middle Sioux (Nakota) and Western Sioux (Lakota) tribes continued to migrate west, where they acquired horses and created an economy based upon the buffalo.

The Nakota (Middle) group generally lived on the prairies east of the Missouri River and acted as a bridge between the Dakota (Eastern) and Lakota (Western) groups. The Nakotas were a cultural bridge as well as a physical one; their unique culture contained elements from both the Lakota and Dakota cultures. The Lakotas, living on the Plains, developed the Plains Indian culture that is most familiar to non-Indians who think about Indian life.

The Sioux's language held them in a loose confederation; anyone speaking a Dakota dialect was an ally. Anyone speaking a different language was automatically an enemy unless a formal peace was arranged. The Dakotas' name means "ally." The word Sioux, on the other hand, has origins that come from outside the Sioux; it is a corruption of an Ojibwe word meaning "enemy." The Sioux lived in groups, or bands, known as tiyospaye, and the larger tribal group to which they belonged was called an oyate. While each group usually had a headman,

The Red Cloud delegation of Oglala Sioux pose for a portrait with their Anglo interpreter. Sioux leader Red Cloud, seated in the center, led a battle over the Bozeman Trail around the time this photograph was taken, in the late 1860s or early 1870s.

A group of Dakota Indians playing a ball game that resembles lacrosse. This nineteenth-century illustration features several tipis that came to represent Sioux and other Plains cultures.

council, and military society, decision making was based on a consensus.

The Lakotas, or Western Sioux, symbolized Plains Indian society. Occupying a large area lying between the Missouri River and Bighorn Mountains and stretching up into Canada, they were buffalo hunters who lived in tipis made of buffalo hides. The Lakotas were a society rich in horses, and the men also hunted other game and fished, while the women gathered additional foods based upon what was available and were skilled at beadwork. The men belonged to military societies, which were responsible for policing the people, overseeing the buffalo hunt, and warring with enemies. Their spiritual life was rich and played an integral part of their daily lives. It is therefore somewhat ironic that it is an event that takes place yearly, the annual Sun Dance, in which dancers sacrifice flesh in ritual prayer, that is most well known among non-Natives.

Of all the nations affected by the endless invasions of European and Euro-American settlers, the Siouan Nations resisted most persistently and effectively. They began negotiating treaties with the United States government in the early 1800s. Constant broken promises and the willful U.S. invasion of tribal lands launched a series of armed conflicts between the Siouan Nations and the United States government.

The Sioux Wars (1862–1877) included numerous battles and confrontations. The Minnesota Uprising (1862) occurred when the Santee Dakotas, goaded beyond endurance by cheating government agents, traders, and settlers who robbed them of their lands, killed more than 350 whites under the leadership of Little Crow in a desperate attempt to reclaim their land. As a result, 38 Indians were publicly hanged in a mass execution in Mankato, and the Santee were forced westward.

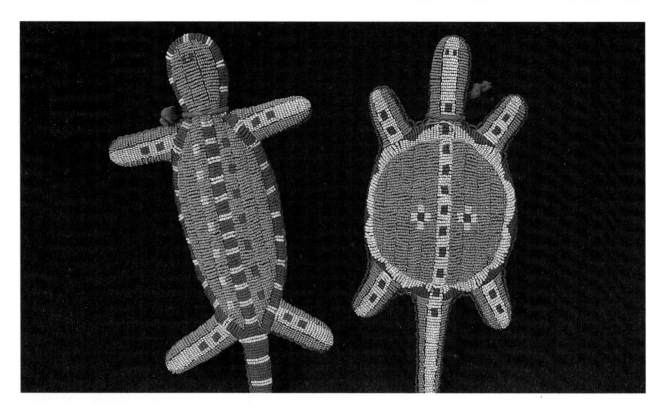

Two examples of Sioux crafts from the late 1800s: beaded leather umbilical cord bags fashioned in the forms of a lizard and a turtle.

From 1865 to 1867, Red Cloud, an Oglala chief, led the Sioux in an offensive to stop the building of the Bozeman Trail. After the Fetterman Massacre, in which more than eighty U.S. soldiers were trapped and killed near Fort Phil Kearney, the Second Treaty of Fort Laramie was signed, in which the United States ceded the area of South Dakota west of the Missouri River to the Lakotas and abandoned their attempt to establish the Bozeman Trail.

This treaty was short lived, however, once gold was discovered in the Black Hills of South Dakota in the 1870s. Thousands of miners, disregarding the Second Treaty of Fort Laramie, entered the Sioux reservation. Hostilities resumed as the Lakota defended their territory, and the U.S. military was soon engaged. During the 1876 Sun Dance, Sitting Bull envisioned many dead U.S. soldiers. Later that same year, the Lakotas and Cheyennes turned back General George Crook's troops at Rosebud and went on to vanquish Lieutenant Colonel George Armstrong Custer's troops at the famous Battle of the Little Bighorn.

Despite these significant victories, the relentless attacks of the United States military soon drove the majority of the Siouan Nations onto reservations, where the confinement, starvation rations, and inability to continue their traditional hunting and trade economy created a climate of misery and despair. Sitting Bull and Crazy Horse each refused to surrender with their people and fled the Black Hills to barely survive a bitter winter. The following spring, Crazy Horse arrived at the Red Cloud agency in force, with all his people and their horses. It was said that no surrender ever looked so victorious. Sitting Bull escaped to Canada, where he lived in exile for years. He returned to the United States, served a prison term, and settled at the Standing Rock agency to continue his political agitation.

A revitalization movement, known as the Ghost Dance Movement, reached the Sioux in the 1880s, leading the people to believe that they would return to their traditional lifestyle, the buffalo would return, and the white people would disappear. The spread of this movement alarmed the U.S. government, which sent in troops to quell the ringleaders. The ultimate resolution occurred when the government troops participated in a sickening massacre of Indian men, women, and children at Wounded Knee in 1890.

The Siouan Nations have continued their resistance, struggling to maintain their cultural heritage and political autonomy and attempting to regain their traditional lands, most notably the Black Hills. They have continued to be politically active in the United States, pursuing legislation in Congress and restitution in the courts. A symbol of continuing resistance was the seizure and occupation at the town of Wounded Knee (1973) by Dakotas and others in the American Indian Movement in order to publicize civil rights grievances.

The Sioux population in 1990 exceeded sixty-nine thousand in the United States. The largest concentration of people can be found on the six reservations in South Dakota; other states containing large Siouan populations include North Dakota, Minnesota, Montana, and California. The people continue to foster traditional Sioux culture in many different arenas and have promoted local educational reform with the founding of several Indian community colleges.

— M. A. Stout

SEE ALSO:
Black Hills; Bozeman Trail, or the Battle of a Hundred Slain; Crazy Horse; Crook, George; Custer, George Armstrong; Ghost Dance Religion; Little Bighorn, Battle of the; Red Cloud; Rosebud Reservation; Siouan Languages; Sitting Bull; Sun Dance; Wounded Knee (1890); Wounded Knee, Confrontation at (1973); Wovoka.

SUGGESTED READINGS:

Biolsi, Thomas. *Organizing the Lakota: The Political Economy of the New Deal on the Pine Ridge and Rosebud Reservations.* Tucson: University of Arizona Press, 1992.

Brown, Dee. *Bury My Heart at Wounded Knee.* New York: Holt, Rinehart and Winston, 1970.

Gump, James O. *The Dust Rose Like Smoke: The Subjugation of the Zulu and the Sioux.* Lincoln: University of Nebraska Press, 1994.

Lazarus, Edward. *Black Hills, White Justice: The Sioux Nation Versus the United States, 1775 to the Present.* New York: HarperCollins, 1991.

McGregor, James H. *The Wounded Knee Massacre: From the Viewpoint of the Sioux.* Rapid City, SD: Fenwyn Press, 1993, © 1940.

Robinson, Charles M. *A Good Year to Die: The Story of the Great Sioux War.* New York: Random House, 1995.

Utley, Robert M. *The Last Days of the Sioux Nation.* New Haven: Yale University Press, 1963.

———. *The Lance and the Shield: The Life and Times of Sitting Bull.* New York: Holt, 1993.

An Oglala tribal representative makes a point at a meeting between U.S. President Bill Clinton and a group of tribal leaders at the White House in Washington, D.C., in 1994.

SIOUX LITERATURE, CONTEMPORARY

Both historically and in recent times, the various peoples of the Sioux have produced an impressive assortment of leaders, fighters, activists, and spokespersons for Native issues. It is not at all surprising that they have also made significant contributions to the literary community as writers of fiction, poetry, and nonfiction, much of it taking to the world of letters the same issues that have consumed Sioux political and military leaders.

Sioux author, professor, and attorney Vine Deloria, Jr., has been one of the most articulate advocates for the recognition of Indian political and religious rights. Born at Standing Rock on the Pine Ridge Reservation, South Dakota, in 1933, he holds degrees in divinity from the Lutheran School of Theology and in law from the University of Colorado. His first book, *Custer Died for Your Sins* (1969), immediately brought him national attention. In short order, he published *We Talk, You Listen: New Tribes, New Turf* (1970), and he has written many books since then.

Sioux poet, author, and professor Elizabeth Cook-Lynn, born on the Crow Creek Reservation in 1930, is a granddaughter of Gabriel Renville, a linguist who helped develop Dakota dictionaries. A Dakota speaker herself, Cook-Lynn has gained prominence as a professor, editor, poet, and scholar. She is emeritus professor of American and Indian studies at Eastern Washington State University, and, in 1985, she became a founding editor of *Wicazo Sa Review*, a biannual scholarly journal for Native American studies professionals. Her book of poetry, *Then Badger Said This*, and her short fiction in such journals as *Prairie Schooner*, *South Dakota Review*, *The Greenfield Review*, and *Sun Tracks*, has established her as a leader among American Indian creative voices.

Virginia Driving Hawk Sneve, a Rosebud Sioux, is the author of eight children's books and other works of historical nonfiction for adults. In 1992, she won the Native American Prose Award from the University of Nebraska Press for her book *Closing the Circle*. Sneve works as a guidance counselor for the school system in Rapid City, South Dakota.

Oglala Sioux Robert L. Perea, born in Wheatland, Wyoming, in 1944, is half Chicano and a graduate of the University of New Mexico. He has published short stories in anthologies such as *Mestizo: An Anthology of Chicano Literature* and *The Remembered Earth*. In 1992, Perea won the inaugural Louis Littlecoon Oliver Memorial Prose Award from his fellow creative writers and poets in the Native Writers' Circle of the Americas for his short story, "Stacey's Story."

Philip H. Red-Eagle, Jr., a Wahpeton-Sisseton Sioux, is a founding editor of *The Raven Chronicles*, a multicultural journal of literature and the arts in Seattle, which has won Washington State Bumbershoot Awards for literary excellence. In 1993, Red-Eagle followed Perea in winning the Louis Littlecoon Oliver Memorial Prose Award for his then-unpublished novel *Red Earth*, which is drawn from his experiences in the Vietnam War.

Fellow Seattle resident and Sioux poet Tiffany Midge, who is enrolled at Standing Rock Reservation, followed Red-Eagle in 1994 by capturing the Diane Decorah Memorial Poetry Award from the Native Writers' Circle of the Americas for her book-length poetry manuscript, *Diary of a Mixed-Up Half-Breed*. Also in 1994, Susan Power, who, like Midge, is enrolled at Standing Rock, gained national attention with the publication of her first novel, *The Grass Dancer*.

SEE ALSO:
Siouan Nations.

SIOUX UPRISING (1862)

Under the terms of a treaty signed with the United States government in 1851, the Minnesota Sioux (Santee) ceded tribal lands and moved onto reservations, where the government was to pay them a certain amount of money and provide food and other supplies. By the early 1860s, however, with the outbreak of the U.S. Civil War, the government fell so far behind in providing promised food supplies and payment of annuities that many Santees were starving. By August 1862, the situation was so desperate that Santees from the Upper Agency (the northern part of the reservation) broke into a government warehouse and took enough pork and flour to feed their families. Santees under the jurisdiction of the Lower Agency, who also were starving, requested emergency rations. Indian agent Thomas Galbraith flatly refused to supply the food, telling the Santees to "eat grass or their own dung." The desperation of the starving, combined with Galbraith's insult, fueled the Great Sioux Uprising of 1862.

Little Crow, then about sixty years old, led the uprising, which began during the early hours of August 18, 1862, with strikes on outlying farms. The Indians quickly killed several hundred settlers. Individuals with whom the Indians had specific grievances (such as the Indian trader Andrew Myrick) were found slain with grass stuffed in their mouths. After three days of intensive raiding, reinforcements joined U.S. troops already in the area, driving the Sioux back slowly, under orders from President Abraham Lincoln to quell the uprising by any means. "Necessity knows no law," Lincoln reportedly told army commanders in the area. Colonel Henry Hopkins Sibley of the Third Minnesota Volunteer Regiment issued orders to "destroy everything they own and drive them out into the plains." "They are to be treated as maniacs or wild beasts," he said.

The Santees killed more than 700 settlers and 100 soldiers before army units drove them onto the Plains. A large number of Santees who had not taken a direct role in the uprising stayed in Minnesota. They expected to be treated as neutrals, but the settlers' wrath fell on them as well. "Exterminate the wild beasts," clamored Jane Swisshelm, editor of the *St. Cloud Democrat*. After the uprising was quelled, a military court condemned 303 of 392 imprisoned Santees to death by hanging. President Lincoln demanded a review of the sentences and cut the number to be executed to 38. Lincoln asserted that each of them had taken part in the massacre, raped women, or both.

The thirty-eight Santees died on a single scaffold at Fort Mankato on December 26, 1862. William J. Dudley, who lost two children to the Santees during the massacre, cut the rope that hung the Santees in the largest mass hanging in United States history: "His knife flashed clean and sure, the traps dropped, and a low, growling roar rose from the grim lips of the soldiers and settlers who watched. The kicking, flailing bodies dangl[ed] grotesquely in the chill December air."

The bodies of the executed men were removed from their mass grave after nightfall by medical doctors, who used them as laboratory specimens. Army units trailed the Santees who had escaped Minnesota to the Badlands of South Dakota. On August 4, 1864, Sibley's forces killed more than five hundred Santee warriors in a single day. A dwindling number of survivors moved westward and took shelter with the Cheyennes. They forged an alliance, which Lt. Colonel George A. Custer would face at the Little Bighorn River a dozen years later.

Little Crow escaped Sibley's raids but was later shot by a farmer (some say the farmer's son made the shot) as he gathered berries. The farmer did not know until later that he had ended the life of the chief who started the Great Sioux Uprising. The Minnesota legislature voted the farmer a $500 reward.

SEE ALSO:
Custer, George Armstrong; Little Bighorn, Battle of the; Little Crow; Minnesota; Siouan Nations.

SITTING BULL (c. 1831–1890)

Sitting Bull (Tatanka-Iyotanka) was a greatly respected spiritual, military, and political leader of the Hunkpapa Lakota of the northern Plains. He was a man of many abilities, and, above all, he was fiercely devoted to the welfare of his people.

Sitting Bull is estimated to have been born around 1831, into a family of great distinction. Among many Plains' tribes, skill in hunting is nurtured from a very young age. Sitting Bull killed his first buffalo at ten years old and gained a reputation as a fine rider and shooter. By the age of fourteen, Sitting Bull had counted his first coup (touched an enemy in battle) and had undergone his first vision quest. In his middle twenties, he became a leader of the Strong Heart Warrior Society—a distinguished club among the Lakotas.

With the growing presence of settlers, the 1850s brought the beginnings of conflict to the inhabitants of the Plains. Sitting Bull, however, did not participate in confrontations with non-Native settlers until 1863, when the settlers' invasion of

A hand-colored, full-length profile photograph of Sitting Bull featuring the Sioux leader in regalia.

Hunkpapa hunting grounds threatened the Hunkpapa people's existence. It was during this time that Sitting Bull made a firm resolution to resist the European-American domination. During the next few years, Sitting Bull and his allies were involved in several skirmishes and battles with the U.S. Army. And it was around this time that Sitting Bull became a military as well as spiritual leader of his people.

When gold was discovered in the Black Hills in 1874, and miners began illegally flooding the area in defiance of the 1868 Treaty of Fort Laramie—which promised the land to the Lakotas—tensions grew even greater between the Indians and the invaders. The government ordered the "hostile" bands to go to the Sioux agencies attached to the reservations, but Sitting Bull and his allies refused to comply.

To enforce the order, the government planned a full military attack to pin down the Indians in the Bighorn Valley. What was unknown to the military was that the largest gathering of Plains Indians, numbering seven to ten thousand and comprising mostly Sioux and Cheyennes—Sitting Bull and his allies among them—were camped at the Little Bighorn River. This confrontation led to what is considered one of the most famous battles in U.S. history, known as the 1876 Battle of the Little Bighorn, in which Lt. Colonel George Armstrong Custer's army was defeated and Custer himself lost his life.

After the Little Bighorn victory, Sitting Bull and a number of his followers fled to Canada to escape the government's orders to surrender. Nearing starvation and exhaustion, however, Sitting Bull's band was finally forced to retreat back to the United States and give themselves up on July 19, 1881.

During the years 1885 to 1886, Sitting Bull traveled with William Cody's Wild West Show and then spent his remaining years on the Standing Rock Reservation in South Dakota. On December 15, 1890, a Bureau of Indian Affairs (BIA) agent ordered Sitting Bull's arrest for his alleged involvement in the Ghost Dance religion, which the BIA thought to be an Indian uprising. A confrontation with U.S. troops occurred, leaving several hundred people dead of gunshot wounds, including Sitting Bull.

SEE ALSO:
Black Hills; Buffalo Bill Cody; Buffalo Bill's Wild West Show; Bureau of Indian Affairs; Coup Sticks, or Counting Coup; Custer, George Armstrong; Fort Laramie Treaty of 1868; Ghost Dance Religion; Siouan Nations; Wounded Knee (1890).

SIX NATIONS

SEE Iroquois Confederacy.

SKENANDOAH (c. 1710–1816)

An Oneida, Skenandoah ("Deer") lived at Oneida Castle, New York. He supported the British in the French and Indian War (1754–1763) but switched his allegiance to the colonists during the American Revolution. Little is known of his early life or the early years of his chieftainship, except that he became a committed campaigner against alcohol after he got drunk and was robbed while sleeping on a street in Albany, New York. As an adult, Skenandoah was exceptionally tall (about six foot, three inches, or nearly two meters) and known for his grace of manner.

Although Skenandoah asserted the Oneidas' official neutrality at the beginning of the American Revolution, along with the Tuscaroras, he supplied warriors and intelligence to the Continental Army. As Washington's army shivered in the snow at Valley Forge, Skenandoah's Oneidas carried baskets of corn to the starving troops. Washington later named the Shenandoah Valley after the Oneida chief in appreciation of his support. During September of 1778, Skenandoah supplied a key warning to residents of German Flats, near Albany, that their settlements were about to be raided by the British with their Iroquois allies under Joseph Brant. The settlers were thus able to get out of the area in time, but their homes and farms were burned and their livestock captured.

After the revolution, Skenandoah continued to serve as a principal chief of the Oneidas and signed several treaties on their behalf. Skenandoah was a close friend of the missionary Samuel Kirkland

and was buried, at Skenandoah's request, next to Kirkland at the Hamilton College cemetery in Clinton, New York, after having lived to the extraordinary age of about 110.

SEE ALSO:

American Revolution; Brant, Joseph; Iroquois Confederacy; Oneida; Tuscarora.

S'KLALLUM (KLALLUM)

SEE Port Gamble Klallum.

SKOKOMISH

The Skokomish Reservation is located in Mason County in Washington State, with its tribal headquarters in Shelton, Washington. The reservation contains 4,987 acres (2,020 hectares). The tribe has 1,025 enrolled members, with 431 living on-reservation. Skokomish means "people of the river."

The Skokomish Reservation was created on January 26, 1855, by the Point-No-Point Treaty. The treaty was ratified by the United States Congress on March 25, 1859, and the reservation was enlarged by executive order on February 25, 1874. The Skokomish tribe accepted the Indian Reorganization Act in 1934 and a tribal constitution in 1938. The Skokomish Tribal Council is the sovereign governing body of the tribe and consists of seven members who serve four-year terms. The Skokomish have treaty fishing rights and are represented on the Northwest Indian Fisheries Commission.

Traditionally, the Skokomish were recognized as expert carvers and basket makers. When young boys and girls showed an interest and a natural talent in woodcarving or basketry, they were encouraged to develop their skills by serving as an apprentice to a master artisan. Instructed to watch and copy the work of the master, the novices were taught to gather and prepare necessary materials and to make the tools needed for their art. When students became accomplished enough, they were allowed to work on major projects. Young carvers worked on totem poles with the master carving one side, and the student copying the design on the other side. In addition, the young artist would seek a spirit helper through ceremonial practices, since it was believed that to be truly successful, one must have spiritual support. An especially talented artist was believed to have been spiritually endowed with his or her gift. Master carvers and basket makers were highly regarded and enjoyed a prestigious place in Skokomish society. They received payment in food, clothing, and other items for their work.

After contact with Europeans, many elements of Skokomish culture changed, especially during the "forced-schooling" period when Skokomish children were required to attend boarding schools and were punished for attempting to maintain their tribal beliefs, customs, and language. Still, many Skokomish managed to maintain a sense of their special culture, and they do so to this day. In recent years, in fact, the Skokomish Tribe began a special art project to redevelop carving and basketry, two of the gifts that they have long brought to the Pacific Northwest.

SEE ALSO:

Indian New Deal (Indian Reorganization Act of); Washington Coast and Puget Sound Indians, History of.

SLAVES, INDIANS AS

The enslavement of Native Americans, first by European settlers and conquerors and later by Euro-Americans, occurred in a variety of forms and under a number of guises. Although slavery never achieved the enormous proportions among Native people of the Americas as it did among Africans who were kidnapped and taken to the Western Hemisphere for the purpose of becoming human "property," its use against Native Americans was equally cruel in its purposefulness and harsh in its effect on its victims.

Native people of the Americas were first enslaved by the Spanish, starting with Christopher Columbus, the Italian navigator who sailed to the Western Hemisphere on behalf of Spain in 1492. It did not take long for Columbus to marshal the resources necessary to transport Indians back to

This detail of a Diego Rivera mural on the Governor's Palace in the Mexican state of Oaxaca shows the building of a Spanish church in Mexico. The Spanish clergy is shown pursuing their own privileged way of life, while the Native population performs various manual tasks in a condition of virtual slavery.

Europe: Following his first journey to the so-called New World, Columbus brought about five hundred Native people back to Spain as slaves. Meanwhile, back in the Americas, Europeans put Indians to work as slaves excavating mines and tending crops of grain, cotton, and sugar as soon as the early 1500s. As the years passed, more Indians were shipped back to Europe, often to be displayed as "converted Christians," and many were sold into slavery there. By 1525, slave hunters were setting sail for the "New World" in hopes of capturing Natives to sell on the slave market in Europe.

Many famous European explorers and conquerors, such as Francisco Vásquez de Coronado and Hernando de Soto, were also famous for stealing food and riches from the Indians and enslaving them for the purpose of carrying their goods and serving as guides to other Native villages. The Europeans would then raid these villages and begin anew their plundering of Indian communities for treasure and human labor. These explorers were able to subdue Native people through a show of great force using weapons and military tactics with which the Indians were unfamiliar. These raids often resulted in the massacre of hundreds and even thousands of Indian warriors, leaving the surviving members of the community—mostly women and children—doomed to a life of slavery.

By the mid-1600s, slavery had been outlawed in Spain, but numerous exceptions and loopholes in the law allowed for various types of slavery to persist. For example, prisoners taken during war could be enslaved, and the Spaniards, who had little trouble starting wars with Native people, could thus take prisoners and use them as slaves.

Spanish colonizers were not the only Europeans in America to force Natives into a life of involuntary servitude. As early as 1614, the English were capturing hundreds of Indian people in America and selling them on the slave market in Spain. As with the Spanish, the English usually took survivors of massacres—again, mostly women and children—to sell into slavery. In many of these cases, the enslavement of Native people was justified not only on military grounds but on religious grounds as well. In Spain, citizens and political leaders alike were often inspired by certain declarations from the Catholic Church that seemed to justify the enslavement of other human beings. These declarations, called papal bulls, were statements of church policy that came directly from the pope. Some papal bulls of the day supported the notion that any land which is inhabited by non-Christians was to be considered uninhabited and that the non-Christians were to be converted, enslaved, or killed.

In the early 1800s, in the decades just following the founding of the United States, Indians in the southeastern portion of the country often found themselves enslaved if they resisted forced removal from their lands. With the development of mission schools, Indian children were trained to be subservient to wealthier non-Indians. And in some cases, during holidays, Indian children were sent to the homes of wealthy Euro-Americans to perform manual labor.

This type of slavery, while less overtly cruel and less widespread than that perpetrated against Black Americans in the South, was coercive nonetheless. Also, the U.S. government was often involved in helping non-Indians obtain Indian slave labor; the orders to transfer students to private homes were often carried out by the military officers who were managing some of the Indian boarding schools.

Well into the nineteenth century, Indians continued to be forced into service to guide famous explorers, carry loads of food and goods for the explorers, tend crops, clean homes, cook, and do other types of manual labor that non-Indians would not do for themselves. There are also reports that punishment for those who misbehaved ranged from beatings to imprisonment in stockades and even death. By the late 1800s, it had become a common practice for settlers and traders to kidnap Indian children and take them to southern states to be sold into slavery. It was even reported in a California newspaper of the time as a "common practice."

Before slavery of all kinds became contrary to public policy and private practice in the United States, many Native people resisted the attempts by Europeans and European-Americans to capture them and force them into servitude. There are reports that Indian people relied on their intimate knowledge of the land surrounding their communities to outsmart slaveholders and others who came looking for slaves. And in the Southeast, particularly in Florida, at least one Indian nation—the Seminoles—forged a reputation as a haven for escaped African-American slaves and even absorbed many Blacks into their own community.

— S. S. Davis

SEE ALSO:

Boarding Schools; California Missions; Columbus, Christopher; Coronado Expedition; De Soto Expedition; Encomienda; Missions for Indians, Christian; Papal Bull.

SLOAN, THOMAS L. (1863–?)

The first Native American attorney to argue a case before the United States Supreme Court, Thomas L. Sloan was born on May 14, 1863, in St. Louis, Missouri. Sloan was of mixed Omaha and European descent. He lived in Nebraska beginning in 1873, where he attended schools in Richardson County and at the Omaha agency. In 1886, he began attending the Hampton Normal and Agricultural Institute in Virginia, a school providing education to African-American and Native American students.

At Hampton, Sloan was a leader in a number of student organizations and graduated at the top of his class in 1889. Although offered a scholarship to continue his studies at Yale Law School, he chose to read for the law under Hiram Chase, an Omaha attorney. Admitted to the bar in 1891, he and his teacher formed the law firm Chase and Sloan. Sloan's legal work centered around cases involving American Indians. He argued a case before the U.S. Supreme Court on behalf of members of his tribe in 1904.

Sloan became the mayor of Pender, Nebraska, in 1901 and was also elected to the village board of trustees, elected county surveyor, and appointed federal court commissioner in his community. He also owned a productive flour mill in Pender. He served as president of the Society of American Indians, an organization he helped found in 1911 to work on behalf of Native Americans.

By 1913, Sloan had moved to Washington, D.C., where he continued to practice law. President Warren G. Harding later selected him to serve on the Committee of One Hundred to provide advice on American Indian policy. The work of this influential group resulted in the Meriam Report of 1928, a landmark study of the federal government's American Indian policies and programs. Sloan's role in public life was often filled with controversy, as he fought with other politicians and leaders over the issues of the day.

SEE ALSO:

Dietz, Angel de Cora; Hampton Institute; Meriam, Lewis; Picotte-LaFlesche, Susan.

SMALLPOX

Smallpox was the single deadliest disease to afflict Native Americans after contact with Europeans in North America began with the first voyage of Columbus more than five hundred years ago. The combination of smallpox and other imported diseases (such as whooping cough and scarlet fever) caused American Indian populations to decline more rapidly than any other factor, including alcoholism and direct conquest.

Countless Native cultures have been decimated by smallpox, a horrible disease by any measure. During the 1630s, Massachusetts Bay governor William Bradford used these words to describe smallpox victims in the simple act of trying to roll over on a straw mat: "For want of linen and bedding and other helps, they fall into a lamentable condition as they lie on their hard mats, the pox breaking and mattering, and running into one another, their skin cleaving by reason thereof to the mats they lie on. When they turn them, a whole side will flay off at once, at it were, and they will be all of a gore blood, most fearful to behold. And then being very sore, what with cold and other distempers, they die like rotten sheep."

Spanish chronicler Bernal Díaz del Castillo stood atop a great temple in the Aztec capital of Tenochtitlán and described causeways eight paces wide teeming with thousands of people and of crossing lakes and channels dotted by convoys of canoes. He said that Spanish soldiers who had been to Rome or Constantinople told Díaz that "for . . . population, they have never seen the like." Within a decade, epidemics of smallpox and other diseases carried by the conquistadores had killed at least half of the Aztecs. One of the Aztec chroniclers who survived wrote, "Almost the whole population suffered from racking coughs and painful, burning sores."

The plague followed the Spanish conquest as it spread in roughly concentric circles from the islands of Hispaniola and Cuba to the mainland of present-day Mexico. Bartolomé de Las Casas, the Roman Catholic priest who criticized Spanish treatment of Native peoples, said that, when the first visitors happened upon Hispanola, it was a beehive of people. Within one lifetime, the forests grew silent. Within thirty years of Hernán Cortés's arrival in Mexico, the Native population had fallen from about twenty-five million to roughly six million.

A century later, entering North America, the Puritans often wondered why the lands on which they settled, which otherwise seemed so bountiful, had been wiped clean of their Native inhabitants. Four years before the *Mayflower* landed, a plague of smallpox had swept through Native villages along the coast of the area the settlers would rename New England. John Winthrop, the first governor of the Massachusetts Bay Colony, admired abandoned Native cornfields and then declared that God had provided the epidemic that killed the people who had tended them as an act of divine providence: "God," he said, "hath hereby cleared our title to this place."

The virulence of the plagues from Europe may be difficult to comprehend in our time. Even in Europe, where immunities had developed to many of the most serious diseases, one in seven people died in typical smallpox epidemics. Half the children born in Europe at the time of contact never reached the age of fifteen, and life expectancy on both sides of the Atlantic averaged thirty-five years.

As settlement of North America spread westward, Native people learned to fear the sight of the honeybee. These "English flies" usually colonized areas about 100 miles (161 kilometers) in advance of the frontier; the first sight of them came to be regarded as a harbinger of Europeans—and of death by imported disease.

SEE ALSO:

Aztec; Cortés, Hernán; Cuba; Demography, Native; Epidemic Diseases; Hispaniola; Las Casas, Bartolomé de; Massachusetts; Mexico, Indigenous Peoples of; Spain.

SMITH, JOHN

SEE Pocahontas.

SMOKESHOPS, RESERVATION

SEE Tobacco.

SNAKE DANCE

The Snake Dance represents a single event in the Hopi cycle of ceremonies, but no other ceremonial occurrence has captured the imagination of outsiders since it was first reported in the late nineteenth century. The Snake Dance has the dubious distinction of being the most photographed, sketched, and publicized Native American ritual ever recorded. By the early 1900s, after the Santa Fe Railway published an account in 1895 designed to attract visitors to Arizona, non-Indian spectators began to outnumber Indians.

The Hopi could never have anticipated the impact of Lieutenant John G. Bourke's written account, published in 1884, nor of anthropologist Jesse Fewkes's descriptions, published from 1894 to 1898. Both men witnessed parts of the ceremony that should never have been recorded and reported. Fewkes admitted in his writing that he entered kivas (underground ceremonial dwellings maintained by clans) that he was asked not to enter and refused to leave when requested. After years of

This news photo, dated 1937, depicts a group of white businessmen, not American Indians, performing a ritual purportedly based on the Hopi Snake Dance in Prescott, Arizona. This event, the seventeenth annual such spectacle performed by a group of white men dressed as Indians and handling live snakes, drew a crowd of five thousand spectators. It lends a bizarre air of truth to the argument that the Snake Dance has been a source of overwhelming fascination to non-Natives and is one of the most photographed and imitated Native rituals known.

unwanted publicity, increasing restrictions were placed upon observers in order to control crowds, and in 1986, the Snake Dance was closed to non-Indian spectators.

The Hopi people live in several different settlements atop Arizona's high mesas. Their communities have existed for thousands of years, and each community celebrates the Snake Dance in its own unique way. In the early nineteenth century, five communities celebrated the dance; today, three villages observe it in rotation. Therefore, details of the ceremony may differ depending upon where the event is taking place.

The elements of this particular ceremony are steeped in the creation account of two Hopi clans. According to this account, a young Hopi man, Tiyo, sought out Spider Woman to act as his guide on a trip to the underworld. In the Snake kiva of the underworld, Tiyo learned what he must do in order to ensure that his land receive rain and his crops prosper. He returned to his village with two maidens from the Snake clan, whom he and his brother married. They began the ceremony that sends snakes to the underworld with their prayers for rain.

The actual ceremony is quite lengthy, with the public Snake Dance occurring on the ninth day. Most of the ceremony takes place in the kivas of the Snake and Antelope societies, or clans. From the day the ceremony is announced, runners bearing plumed prayer sticks go out to place them at special locations. For four days prior to the dance, snakes are hunted in the north, west, south, and east and returned to the Snake kiva.

The Antelope Dance is held in the plaza the day before the Snake Dance. Before sunrise, the Snake Race commences, with the runners carrying produce from the fields into the village. A bower of cottonwood branches is built in the plaza; this is where the snakes will be placed during the dance. On the ninth day, the men prepare for the dance with a washing and purification in the kiva. Similarly, the snakes are washed and purified.

The actual dance involves the ceremonially attired members of both the Snake and Antelope clans. The Snake clan member reaches into the cottonwood bower for a snake, which he places in his mouth, and he dances each snake four times around the plaza before releasing it. Each dancer is accompanied by an Antelope clan member who carries a snake whip, traditionally made from eagle feathers, which is used to distract the snake from coiling and striking. After all the snakes in the bower have been danced around the plaza and set down, the Snake clan members run to plunge their hands into the pile of snakes and race with them in the four directions, to be released as a way of bringing petitions for rain to their kin in the underworld. After this, the dancers are again purified, and the feasting begins.

SEE ALSO:
Arizona; Hopi; Kiva; Spider Woman.

SNEVE, VIRGINIA DRIVING HAWK (1933–)

Virginia Driving Hawk Sneve is a Native novelist and editor. Of Brulé Sioux ancestry, she was born in Rosebud, South Dakota, in 1933 and earned bachelor and master of education degrees from the University of South Dakota. She taught and was a guidance counselor before becoming an editor for Brevet Press of Sioux Falls. Sneve is a member of the Rosebud Sioux Tribe and has served as a member of the board of directors of the United Sioux Tribes Cultural Arts Council.

Sneve's first novel was *High Elk's Treasure*, published in 1972. In this book, a Brulé Sioux settles on the Dakota Reservation and breeds a herd of horses from one old lame mare. The herd becomes big and famous, but over the years, the herd is diminished until only one filly remains. Joe High Elk, High Elk's great-grandson, hopes to rebuild the herd; a key to making that dream come true is finding "High Elk's treasure," a missing drawing done by Rain-in-the-Face depicting General George Armstrong Custer's death.

Sneve's next novel, *Jimmy Yellow Hawk*, was also published in 1972 and was named best work of the year in the American Indian category by the Interracial Council for Minority Books for Children. Little Jimmy Yellow Hawk is ten years old and wants to earn the respect of his tribe. By becoming a well-known trapper, Jimmy earns everyone's admiration and wins his adult name.

When Thunders Spoke was published in 1974. In this novel, fifteen-year-old Norman Two Bull finds an old coup stick on Butte of Thunders. Norman soon realizes that the coup stick is "wakan" (holy or endowed with special power) when good things start to happen to his family. Norman must make important choices when he faces offers to buy the coup stick.

Betrayed was also published in 1974 and is the historical story of the 1862 Santee Sioux revolt in Minnesota. White Lodge's Santee band takes several women and children hostage, and Charger and his Teton braves barter for the hostages' release.

A year later, *The Chichi Hoohoo Bogeyman* was published. Three American Indian girls are menaced by an evil-looking man whom they name after the dangerous figures in Sioux, Hopi, and non-Native American stories.

In addition to these works, Sneve is also the author of several other nonfiction works about South Dakota history and Dakota Sioux history and knowledge.

SEE ALSO:
Coup Sticks, or Counting Coup; Custer, George Armstrong; Siouan Nations; Sioux Uprising (1862); South Dakota.

SNYDER ACT OF 1921

The Snyder Act of 1921 authorizes the Bureau of Indian Affairs (BIA) to "expend such moneys as Congress may from time to time appropriate, for the benefit, care, and assistance of the Indians throughout the United States."

The act provided broad authorization for a host of federal services to Indians, but these services will only continue for as long as Congress decides to fund them. The act was the first effort by Congress to improve general health care for Indians, authorizing the expenditure of federal funds "for the relief of distress and conservation of health of Indians."

SEE ALSO:
Bureau of Indian Affairs; Indian Health Service.

SOCIAL CONDITIONS, CONTEMPORARY

In some ways, life for Native people living on reservations in the United States and on Canadian reserves has become more difficult at the end of the twentieth century. By 1990, for example, the Pine Ridge Oglala Lakota (Sioux) Reservation in southwest South Dakota had become the poorest area in the United States. Although the situation at Pine Ridge is among the most dramatic instances of the decline in living conditions on reservations, it is worth looking at as an example of what has happened on many reservations.

Pine Ridge—whose inhabitants are descended from Crazy Horse and Red Cloud and live at the site of the 1890 massacre at Wounded Knee and the 1973 confrontation there—is situated in an area that includes three of the United States' poorest counties. Shannon County, which includes the eastern two-thirds of Pine Ridge (nine thousand people of a reservation total of sixteen thousand) was the nation's poorest county in 1989, with a poverty rate of 63.1 percent, up from 44.7 percent in 1979. Ziebach County, comprising the eastern half of the Cheyenne River Reservation north of Pine Ridge, was the seventh poorest county in the United States, with a poverty rate of 51.1 percent in 1989, up from 43.7 percent in 1979. Todd County, in the Rosebud Sioux Reservation east of Pine Ridge, was the tenth poorest in 1989, with a poverty rate of 50.2 percent, up from 43.5 percent in 1979. Per capita income in Shannon County fell 23 percent during the 1980s after adjusting for inflation.

The "poverty line" in 1989 was an annual income of $6,311 for a single person and $12,675 for a family of four. The fact that the poverty rate rose in all ten of the United States' poorest counties between 1979 and 1989 indicates that rural poverty was becoming more intense among all ethnic groups, including Native Americans. The national poverty rate was 14.2 percent in 1989.

By 1989, nearly seven of every ten people in Shannon County were unemployed; virtually the only work came from government agencies and the underground economy. Pine Ridge Village, the largest town on the reservation, had no train, bus, bank, theater, clothing store, or barbershop. Big Bat's, the one major Native-owned business in

A Piscataway woman cares for her baby, who was born only an hour before this photo was taken. Despite the persistence of poverty in the lives of most Indian people, many Native communities have taken steps to ensure strong educations and the hope of a brighter future for their children.

Two young women sell Navajo jewelry along a highway in Monument Valley, Arizona.

Pine Ridge, was taken to court thirteen times by European-American land- and business owners who tried to prevent its opening. Meanwhile, the pervasiveness of poverty was shattering families and causing people to turn to alcohol and other drugs.

Infant mortality at Pine Ridge is twenty-nine deaths per one thousand children, three times the national average. The death rate from homicide is also three times the national average. The people of Pine Ridge die from alcoholism at ten times the national rate, not taking into account the damage caused by fetal alcohol syndrome. The death rate from adult diabetes is four times the average. The tribal housing authority had a waiting list of two thousand families for subsidized lodging, at least a quarter of the people on the reservation.

John Yellow Bird Steele, chairman of the Oglala Sioux Tribal Council in 1992, advocated construction of three casinos to alleviate unemployment and provide private industry on the reservation. However, the Wounded Knee chapter of the American Indian Movement believes that gambling will drive poor people on the reservation further into alcoholism and debt. "That's genocide," said Gary Rowland of Wounded Knee AIM. In the midst of

deepening poverty and divisiveness, however, a tribal consensus to upgrade education produced improved schools and a number of well-kept school buildings. Since 1970, the tribe has gradually taken over administration of most reservation schools from the Bureau of Indian Affairs (BIA).

The indications of poverty in South Dakota were nearly duplicated in neighboring states. In Nebraska, unemployment on the Omaha Reservation stood at 71 percent in the late 1980s; among the Santee Sioux, unemployment was 55 percent, compared to 65 percent among the Winnebagos. Nationwide, the civilian unemployment rate among Native Americans on reservations was about 30 percent in 1990. Unemployment on the Navajo Nation, with its workforce of 87,000 people the largest reservation in the United States, was 29.5 percent.

Nationwide, Native Americans' income was falling in 1990 as measured against all other ethnic groups in the United States. According to the census bureau, the median household income for Native Americans (inflation-adjusted) fell from $20,541 in 1980 to $20,025 in 1990, while the same figure for European-Americans rose from $29,632 to $31,435. The percentage of Native Americans defined as living below the poverty line increased from 27.5 percent in 1980 to 30.9 percent in 1990, while the percentage for Euro-Americans rose from 9.4 percent to 9.8 percent. In 1990, the census bureau found that 29.5 percent of African-Americans, 14.1 percent of Asian-Americans, and 25.3 percent of Hispanic-Americans lived in poverty. In 1989, the Children's Defense Fund found that 66 percent of Native American children in Minneapolis were in families with incomes below the poverty line.

Social conditions were no better in Canada by about 1990. According to the Canadian Assembly of First Nations, of 466,337 Native people in Canada, about 60 percent are on welfare; the average family income ($10,382 Canadian, or about $7,800 U.S. at 1994 exchange rates) is only half of the national average. Unemployment averages between 70 percent and 90 percent on most reserves, and the number of suicides by men is five times the national average. Almost half of the homes on reserves have no central heating.

Although many statistics indicate that Indians experienced intensifying poverty at the end of the twentieth century, other indicators reveal improvement in some areas of health and welfare. For example, the Indian Health Service (IHS) reports that the homicide rate for Native Americans (per 100,000 people) declined from 23.8 in 1955 to 14.1 in 1988, as the rate for all races in the United States increased from 4.8 to 9.0 per 100,000. While 57 percent of African-American homicide victims and 47 percent of Euro-American homicide victims were killed with guns between 1966 and 1988, only 29 percent of Indians were murdered with firearms; 32 percent were killed with knives. Deaths from alcoholism among Indians declined from 56.6 per 100,000 in 1969 to 33.9 in 1988, while the rate for all races in the United States declined only slightly, from 7.7 to 6.3 per 100,000. Put another way, in 1969, the alcoholism death rate for American Indians and Alaska Natives was 7.4 times that of the general population. In two decades, that figure fell to 5.4 times that of the general population, according to the IHS.

During the last years of the twentieth century, many Native people's quality of life declined because of pollution on or near their reservations. For example, the Akwesasne (St. Regis Mohawk) Reservation, which straddles the U.S.–Canadian border in New York, Quebec, and Ontario, has been so badly polluted that its residents cannot eat fish from nearby rivers or produce from some of their own gardens.

— B. E. Johansen

A scene combining natural splendor and a life of hard times in a Paiute village in Utah.

SOCKALEXIS, LOUIS (1871–1913)

Louis Sockalexis, a Penobscot, is legendary for his natural talent, his .313 lifetime batting average, and his status as one of big league baseball's earliest Native Americans. Sadly, he is also known for the meteoric decline of his career, a decline driven largely by alcoholism.

Lou Sockalexis was born on October 24, 1871, into the Penobscot community of Old Town, Maine. Catcher Mike "Doc" Powers lured Sockalexis to Holy Cross College in 1895 and 1896 and then to Notre Dame for 1897. Sockalexis signed with Cleveland to join them after the school year; when Sockalexis and a friend were jailed for vandalism, Cleveland Spiders manager Oliver Tebeau posted his bail.

Sockalexis debuted as a professional on April 22, 1897. Amid racial taunts and "Indian" cheers, he played sixty-six games that year, batting .338 with 42 RBI (runs batted in) in 278 at-bats, an on-base percentage of .385, and stealing 16 bases. However, alcohol ruined him, and by mid-August, he was benched. During the next two years, he hit .224 and .273 respectively in twenty-eight total games. Until 1903, he played for a series of New England minor league teams. The obscurity of his later years is punctuated by reports of drunkenness and beggary.

He died on Christmas Eve, 1913, in Burlington, Maine. At the time, the Cleveland team, now in the American League, had no permanent nickname. Following the 1914 season, its fans voted for "Indians," intending to honor the enigmatic outfielder. Baseball writer Luke Salisbury's novel *The Cleveland Indian: The Legend of King Saturday* (1992) loosely parallels the life of Louis Sockalexis.

Penobscot athlete Lou Sockalexis, second from the right, is photographed with a group of non-Native athletes, probably during his college years in the 1890s.

SEE ALSO:
Alcoholism; Baseball; Penobscot.

SOUTH CAROLINA

One of the original thirteen English colonies in America, South Carolina became the eighth U.S. state on May 23, 1788. For centuries before the earliest contact with Spanish and later French explorers in the 1500s, present-day South Carolina was home to many of the Indian peoples that comprised today's southeastern United States. One of these groups, the Cherokee, was a thriving nation whose lands covered 135,000 square miles (351,000 square kilometers) over eight present-day U.S. states, including South Carolina, at the time of contact with Spain's de Soto expedition. By the mid-1800s, most southeast Native people had been removed to Indian Territory (Oklahoma).

Today, South Carolina has one Native community located on a reservation—the Catawbas in Rock Hill. The 1990 census lists 8,246 Indians as state residents, ranking South Carolina fortieth among states in Native population.

SOUTH DAKOTA

South Dakota became the fortieth U.S. state on November 2, 1889. Dakota is a Sioux word that means "alliance of friends." In addition to providing South Dakota with its name, American Indians have been involved with this region in many other ways. Archaeological evidence indicates that Indians have lived in the area that is now called South Dakota for thousands of years. The earliest Indians to live in the region were the early Paleo-Indian hunters. In about 500 C.E., people from the Mound Builder Culture occupied sites along the Big Sioux River. In about 1100 C.E. the Arikara people arrived in the area and began building fortified villages along the Missouri River.

The first Europeans to enter the region were the French explorers François and Louis Joseph La Verendyre, who claimed the land for France in 1742. After 1742, Sioux Indians began moving into South Dakota from the west, and Cheyenne Indians began to move southward from the area of present-day North Dakota. These tribes forced the Arikaras farther westward. The first permanent European settlement was established at Yankton in 1862.

In 1874, a party led by Lt. Colonel George Arm-

Federal troops block a street near Wounded Knee, South Dakota, the scene of a 1973 Indian protest that turned violent. South Dakota has a long history of conflict between Native people and the U.S. government.

strong Custer discovered gold in the Black Hills region of the state, and new towns such as Deadwood sprang up. Treaties that had been set forth with the Sioux were violated, and conflicts between settlers and the Sioux intensified. Sioux and Cheyenne warriors won a great victory over Custer and his troops at the Battle of the Little Bighorn in 1876, but soon after the battle, most of the Sioux leaders, such as Red Cloud and Spotted Tail—or Sinte Gleska—surrendered and moved their people to reservations. Indian resistance ended after the massacre at Wounded Knee, South Dakota, in 1890.

In 1973, Indian resistance resurfaced when members of the American Indian Movement (AIM) occupied Wounded Knee for ten weeks. The takeover ended in the deaths of several AIM members and two FBI agents.

There currently are nine reservations in South Dakota: Cheyenne River, Crow Creek, Flandreau Santee Sioux, Lower Brule, Pine Ridge, Standing Rock, Lake Traverse (Sisseton), Rosebud, and Yankton. Many of these reservations are very large: Pine Ridge contains 1,780,444 acres (721,080 hectares), Cheyenne River 1,395,905 acres (565,342 hectares), Rosebud 954,572 acres (386,602 hectares), and Standing Rock 847,254 acres (343,138 hectares).

The 1990 U.S. Census lists 50,575 Indians as state residents, which ranks South Dakota tenth among states in Native American population.

SEE ALSO:

American Indian Movement; Arikara; Black Hills; Cheyenne; Custer, George Armstrong; Mound Builders; North Dakota; Pine Ridge Occupation; Red Cloud; Rosebud Reservation; Siouan Nations; Spotted Tail; Wounded Knee (1890); Wounded Knee, Confrontation at (1973).

SOUTHWEST LITERATURE, CONTEMPORARY

Native people of the Southwest are making significant contributions to contemporary literature. Many Navajos have distinguished themselves as poets, and the tribe has produced some of the finest Native American poets. Rex Jim, from Tse Dildo'ii near Rock Point in the Navajo Nation and grand-

son of Hosteen Yellowman, a well-known medicine man, is the first author to have published a volume of poetry in Navajo (without translation) with a major university press, *Ahi'Ni'Nikisheegiizh* (Princeton University Press). Jim's fiction and nonfiction have also been published by Rock Point Community School in the Navajo Nation and include such works as *Naakaiiahgoo Tazhdiya* and *Living from Livestock.*

Elizabeth Woody was born on the Navajo Nation but raised mostly in the Pacific Northwest; her heritage includes Pacific Northwest tribes as well as Navajo. Woody returned to the Southwest to study at the Institute of American Indian Arts in Santa Fe, New Mexico, where she studied both poetry and art. Her first volume of poetry, *Hand into Stone*, won the American Book Award. Her other books include *Luminaries of the Humble* (Sun Tracks Series, University of Arizona Press) and *Seven Hands, Seven Hearts* (Eighth Mountain Press). Woody's poetry has been anthologized in *Returning the Gift* (Sun Tracks Series, University of Arizona Press) and in *Durable Breath* (Salmon Run Press); her short fiction "Home Cooking" has been anthologized in *Talking Leaves* (Dell Publishing); and her nonfiction "Warm Springs" has been anthologized in *Native America* (APA Insights). Woody now teaches at the Institute of American Indian Arts. Her illustrations can be found in Sherman Alexie's *Old Shirts & New Skins* (American Indian Studies, UCLA), and her art has been the subject of a five-week exhibit at the Tula Foundation Gallery in Atlanta, Georgia.

The work of Navajo poet Laura Tohe is widely known. Her volume of poetry *Making Friends with Water* was published by Nosila Press. Her poetry and nonfiction have appeared in such publications as *Nebraska Humanities, Blue Mesa Review,* and *Platte Valley Review.* Tohe received a Ph.D. degree from the University of Nebraska in English literature; she now teaches at the University of Arizona. Tohe's latest project is a children's play for the Omaha Emmy Gifford Children's Theater. Tohe is a mentor in the Wordcraft Circle program and is also a member of its 1994–1996 National Advisory Caucus.

Lucy Tapahonso is originally from Shiprock, New Mexico, in the Navajo Nation. She is the author of four books of poetry, the latest being *Saanii Dahataa* (University of Arizona Press). She is an assistant professor at the University of Kansas at

Lawrence. Recently, *New Mexico Magazine* devoted a feature story to Tapahonso and her poetry.

Della Frank is a Navajo poet who lives and works on the Navajo Nation. Her poetry has appeared in such publications as *Blue Mesa Review* and *Studies in American Indian Literature* and has been anthologized in *Neon Powwow: New Native American Voices of the Southwest* (edited by Anna Lee Walters, Northland Publishing, Flagstaff, Arizona, 1993) and *Returning The Gift* (University of Arizona Press). She is coauthor of *Duststorms: Poems from Two Navajo Women* (Navajo Community College Press).

Navajo author Vee Browne has achieved a national reputation with her retellings of Navajo creation stories. Her books have included *Monster Slayer* and *Monster Birds* (Northland Publishing, Flagstaff, Arizona), as well as a children's biography of Osage international ballet star Maria Tallchief (Modern Curriculum Press, a division of Simon & Schuster) and a volume in a new series of Native American animal stories from Scholastic Books. Her honors have included the prestigious Western Heritage Award in 1990 from the Cowboy Hall of Fame and Western Heritage Center. A guidance counselor by training, Browne makes her home near Chinle, Arizona, in the Navajo Nation. She is active in helping emerging Native writers hone their skills and find outlets for their work, serving as a mentor in the Wordcraft Circle of Native American Mentor & Apprentice Writers. She also serves on the 1994–1996 National Advisory Caucus for Wordcraft Circle.

Rachael Arviso, a Navajo and Zuni, lives and works on the Navajo Reservation; her short fiction has been anthologized in *Neon Powwow*. Esther G. Belini's poetry also appeared in *Neon Powwow*; she received her B.A. degree from the University of California at Berkeley. Other Navajos whose work has been anthologized in *Neon Powwow* include Dan L. Crank, Nancy Maryboy, Irvin Morris, Patroclus Eugene Savino, Brent Toadlena, Gertrude Walters, and Floyd D. Yazzie. Aaron Carr, a Navajo and Laguna Pueblo, has had poetry and stories in *The Remembered Earth: An Anthology of Contemporary Native American Literature* (edited by Geary Hobson, University of New Mexico Press, Albuquerque), in *Sun Tracks*, and in *Planet Quarterly*. Bernadette Chato's work has appeared in *New America* and *The Remembered Earth*. Grey Cohoe's work has appeared in several anthologies, including *Whispering Wind*, *The Remembered Earth*, and *The American Indian Speaks*. Larry Emerson's column "Red Dawn" appeared in a number of Indian newspapers, and his work has been anthologized in *New America* and *The Remembered Earth*. Nia Francisco, who was born at Shiprock and has taught at Navajo Community College, has had her work appear in *Southwest: A Contemporary Anthology*, *College English*, *The Remembered Earth*, *Cafe Solo*, *New America*, and *Southwest Women's Poetry Exchange*.

Geraldine Keams has appeared in several films, including *The Outlaw Josey Wales* and has been published in *Sun Tracks* and *The Remembered Earth*. Jean Natoni has published her work in *The Remembered Earth*, as have Aaron Yava, a Navajo-Hopi, and Genevieve Yazzie. Yava's drawings have also appeared in *Border Towns of the Navajo Nation*, *Man to Send Rain Clouds*, and *A Good Journey*. Yazzie's work has also appeared in *New America*, and she worked on a Navajo-English dictionary project.

Apaches are also making important contributions to Native American literature and the arts. Lorenzo Baca, of Mescalero Apache and Isleta Pueblo heritage, is not only a writer, but is also a performing and visual artist who does fine art, sculpture, video, storytelling, and acting. His poetry has been anthologized in *The Shadows of Light: Poetry and Photography of the Motherlode and Sierras* (Jelm Mountain Publications), in *Joint Effort II: Escape* (Sierra Conservation Center), and in *Neon Powwow: New Native American Voices of the Southwest* (Northland Publishing). His audio recording *Songs, Poems and Lies* was produced by Mr. Coyote Man Productions. An innovative writer, his circle stories entitled "Ten Rounds" in *Neon Powwow* are illustrative of his imagination and capacity to create new forms of poetic expression.

Also in the *Neon Powwow* anthology, Jicarilla Apache creative writers Stacey Velarde and Carlson Vicenti present portraits of Native people in the modern world. Velarde, who has been around horses all of her life and has competed in professional rodeos since the age of thirteen, applies this background and knowledge in her story "Carnival Lights," while Vicenti, in "Hitching" and "Oh Saint Michael," shows how Native people incorporate traditional ways into modern life. White Mountain Apache poet Roman C. Adrian has published

Laguna writer Paula Gunn Allen, photographed in 1996.

cle, he organizes and helps conduct intensive writing workshops where young Native writers from all tribes have an opportunity to hone their creative skills and learn how to publish their work.

Other Apache writers include Lou Cuevas, author of *Apache Legends: Songs of the Wild Dancer* (Naturegraph); Jicarilla Apache scholar Veronica E. Velarde Tiller is the author of *The Jicarilla Apache Tribe* (University of Nebraska Press); and Michael Lacapa, of Apache, Hopi, and Pueblo heritage is the author of *The Flute Player* (Northland Publishing) and *The Mouse Couple* (Northland). Throughout the Apache tribes, the traditional literature and knowledge of the people is also handed down from generation to generation by storytellers who transmit their knowledge orally.

The Pueblos have produced some of the most outstanding contemporary Native literary writers. Two of the first three Lifetime Achievement honorees of the Native Writers' Circle of the Americas have been Pueblos—Simon J. Ortiz (Acoma) and Leslie Marmon Silko (Laguna). In the early 1970s, Ortiz was editor of *Americans Before Columbus*, the newspaper of the Indian Youth Council. In the 1980s, he held official tribal positions as interpreter and first lieutenant governor of Acoma. He has taught at the Institute of American Indian Arts, the University of New Mexico, Navajo Community College, Sinte Gleska College, San Diego State University, the College of Marin, Lewis & Clark College, and Colorado College. He edited one of the most important collections of Native literature, *Earth Power Coming*, published by Navajo Community College Press, and has written many books, among them *From Sand Creek*, *Going for the Rain*, *A Good Journey*, *Fightin': New and Collected Stories*, *The People Shall Continue*, and *Woven Stone*.

Leslie Marmon Silko has also taught at a number of universities, including the University of Arizona and the University of New Mexico. Her work has had a profound influence on the Native liter-

poetry in *Sun Tracks*, *The New Times*, *Do Not Go Gentle*, and *The Remembered Earth*. The late Chiricahua Apache poet Blossom Haozous, of Fort Sill, Oklahoma, was a leader in the bilingual presentation of Apache traditional stories, both orally and in publication. One of the stories, "Quarrel Between Thunder and Wind" was published bilingually in *The Chronicles of Oklahoma*, the quarterly scholarly journal of the Oklahoma Historical Society.

Jose L. Garza, a Coahuilateca and Apache, is not only a leading Native American poet, but a leading Native American educator as well. His poetry has appeared in such publications as *Akwe:kon Journal* (of the American Indian Program at Cornell University), *The Native Sun*, *New Rain Anthology*, *The Wayne Review*, *Triage*, and *The Wooster Review*. Garza is a professor at Edinboro University in Pennsylvania and is a regional coordinator of Wordcraft Circle of Native American Mentor & Apprentice Writers. In Wordcraft Cir-

ary community. Her best-known works are *Ceremony*, *Storyteller*, and *Almanac of the Dead*. Both Ortiz and Silko delivered plenary session speeches at the historic Returning the Gift Conference of North American Native writers at the University of Oklahoma in 1992, a gathering that drew nearly four hundred Native literary writers from throughout the upper Western Hemisphere.

Paula Gunn Allen (Laguna) is another well-known Pueblo author. She edited the anthology *Spider Woman's Granddaughters*. She has also published books of fiction, poetry, and nonfiction. Her titles include *The Woman Who Owned the Shadows*, *Shadow Country*, *Skin and Bones*, *The Sacred Hoop*, and *Studies in American Indian Literatures*. Laguna poet Carol Lee Sanchez has published *Excerpt from a Mountain Climber's Handbook*, *Message Bringer Woman*, and *Conversations from the Nightmare*.

Hopi-Miwok writer Wendy Rose is the coordinator of American Indian studies at Fresno City College and has held positions with the Women's Literature Project of Oxford University Press, the Smithsonian Native Writers' Series, the Modern Language Association Commission on Languages and Literature of the Americas, and the Coordinating Council of Literary Magazines. Her books include *Hopi Roadrunner Dancing*, *Long Division: A Tribal History*, *Academic Squaw: Reports to the World from the Ivory Tower*, *Lost Copper*, *What Happened When the Hopi Hit New York*, *The Halfbreed Chronicles*, *Going to War with All My Relations*, and *Bone Dance*.

Laguna educator Lee Francis, director of the American Indian Internship Program at American University in Silver Springs, Maryland, is also national director of Wordcraft Circle of Native American Mentor & Apprentice Writers and is editor of its newsletter, *Moccasin Telegraph*, and of its quarterly literary journal, *Wordtrails*. In 1994, Francis led a team of Native writers who guest-edited a special Native American literature issue of *Callaloo* for the University of Virginia and Johns Hopkins University Press.

Many other Pueblos are literary writers, including Aaron Carr, Joseph L. Concha, Harold Littlebird, Diane Reyna, Veronica Riley, Joe S. Sando, Laura Watchempino, and Aaron Yava. Some of their best early work appears in *The Remembered Earth*. Some of the most recent work by a new generation of Pueblo literary figures, including Rachael Arviso and Rosemary Diaz, can be found in *Neon Powwow*.

—D. L. Birchfield

SEE ALSO:
Institute of American Indian Arts; Returning the Gift.

SOVEREIGNTY, TRIBAL

SEE Governments, Native; Self-determination; Self-determination Policy; Tribal Sovereignty.

SPAIN

Spain established a presence in the Americas that continues to dominate the language and culture of numerous Latin American nations and large parts of the U.S. Southwest. The Spanish also forged a unique relationship with the Native peoples whose lives they disrupted—and frequently destroyed—and whose lands they colonized. Much of this influence was enforced through sheer military might and the willingness to force that might on indigenous peoples with unrestrained coercion and brutality. Spain also exercised control through the fervor with which Spanish theologians, leaders, and priests pursued the conversion of Native peoples to Christianity.

In 1493, one year after Christopher Columbus's first voyage to the Americas, Pope Alexander IV issued two opinions that shaped European nations' perceptions of their "rights" under church law to discover and occupy territory in this "new" land. In the papal bull (an official document issued by the pope) *Inter Caetera*, Spain was granted all lands not governed by a "Christian prince" as of Christmas Day, 1492. This bull was modified in *Inter Caetera II*, which allocated to Spain all such lands west of a north-south line running 100 leagues (300 miles; 480 kilometers) west of the Azores and Cape Verde Islands. Lands east of that line were reserved for Portugal, the reason that most people in Brazil today speak Portuguese.

The Aztec leader Moctezuma *(left)* welcomes Spanish conquistador Hernán Cortés into Mexico in 1519. As impressed as the Spanish were by Mexico's great civilizations, they were just as taken by the great wealth they found. They were also excited by the thought of sowing the seeds of Christianity among Native peoples in the Americas.

The Spanish monarchy was intrigued with the legal aspects of conquest and very concerned that its Indian policy pass muster with the moral dictates of the Catholic Church. Beginning in about the year 1500 C.E., a debate raged over whether the Native peoples of the New World possessed souls and could be regarded as "human" by European standards. The church, after lengthy debate, found that the Natives did indeed possess souls and that these souls were fit for conversion to Christianity.

Once that question had been settled, European kings, popes, and scholars wrestled with the question of how their nations could "discover" and then "own" lands that were obviously already occupied by the Native peoples of the Americas. Around 1550, the Spanish king Charles V initiated a debate over these questions in which the priest Bartolomé de Las Casas argued for Indian rights and another theologian, Sepulveda, argued against.

But by 1532, the Spanish theologian Francisco de Vitoria (1486–1546) had already written that "the aborigines in question were true owners, before the Spanish came among them, both from the pub-lic and the private point of view." Vitoria wrote in *De Indis et Juri Belli Relectiones* (1532) that "The aborigines undoubtedly had true dominion in both public and private matters . . . neither their princes nor private persons could be despoiled of their property on the ground of their not being true owners." Spain could not, therefore, simply assert ownership of lands occupied by aboriginal people; title by discovery could be justified only if the land was ownerless.

It was Vitoria's opinion that Spain could legally acquire title to Native American land in the so-called New World by conquest resulting from a "just" war, unless the Indians surrendered their title by "free and voluntary choice." A "just war" was precisely defined. War was not to be undertaken on a whim or solely to dispossess the aboriginal inhabitants. As legal scholar Felix Cohen summarized Vitoria's opinions, "So long as the Indians respected the natural rights of the Spaniards, recognized by the law of nations, to travel in their lands and sojourn, trade, and defend their rights therein, the Spaniards could not wage a just war against the Indians and therefore could not claim any rights by conquest."

Vitoria's opinions became the general definition of the Doctrine of Discovery, by which the taking of aboriginal land would be justified for the next four centuries in both Spanish and United States legal practice. The treaty-making procedures of the United States government originally stemmed from Vitoria's 1532 opinion, at least in theory. In practice, treaties were sometimes fraudulent, and wars were undertaken for less than "just" cause.

In the Americas, the Spanish conquistadores observed the dictates of Spanish theologians only in form, not in substance. The cruelties of the conquistadores brought criticism from the Spanish priest Las Casas. While Las Casas was critical of cruelties inflicted upon Native Americans by the Spanish conquest, he still gave Columbus the credit for his God-given navigational skills in crossing the Atlantic so that Europeans could colonize other lands and peoples. However, Las Casas did not want gold; he wanted to convert American Indians to Christianity. His books are filled with graphic detail describing the horrors of the Spanish conquest: "The Spanish found pleasure in inventing all kinds of odd cruelties, the more cruel the better, with which to spill human blood. They built a long gibbet, low enough for the toes to touch the ground and prevent strangling, and hanged thirteen [Natives] at a time in honour of Christ Our Savior and the twelve Apostles. When the Indians were thus alive and hanging, the Spaniards tested their strength and their blades against them, ripping chests open with one blow and exposing entrails, and there were those who did worse. Then straw was wrapped around their torn bodies and they were burned alive. One man caught two children about two years old, pierced their throats with a dagger, then hurled them down a precipice."

One conquistador "sport" was indicative of their sadistic disregard for Native life. It was called "dogging"—the hunting and maiming of Native people by dogs specifically trained to relish the taste of human flesh. According to David E. Stannard,

A legacy of the Spanish presence among Native people in the present-day Southwest United States: a Spanish mission church in Acoma Pueblo, New Mexico.

This detail from a mural by Diego Rivera depicts the oppression of Native people in Mexico at the hands of Spanish colonizers. Here, a group of Indians offers tribute to corrupt Spanish monks in the form of food and personal riches.

some of the dogs were kept as pets by the conquistadores. Vasco Núñez de Balboa's favorite was named Leoncico, or "Little Lion," a cross between a greyhound and a mastiff. On one occasion, Balboa ordered forty Indians dogged at once. "Just as the Spanish soldiers seem to have particularly enjoyed testing the sharpness of their yard-long blades on the bodies of Indian children, so their dogs seemed to find the soft bodies of infants especially tasty," wrote David Stannard in *American Holocaust* (1992). Las Casas also protested the practice of "commending" Indians to *encomenderos* (Spaniards who had been given the legal right to build their wealth on the possessions and labor of Native people)—which resulted in a life free from labor for the encomenderos but virtual slavery for the Natives.

The Caribs, Arawaks, and other Native peoples that Columbus met during his earliest voyages were not the simple independent savages he often imagined them to be. As in many other areas of the Americas, the places that Columbus visited were thickly populated. The island chain including Cuba, Hispaniola, Puerto Rico, and the Bahamas was home to roughly four million people in 1492. The Native peoples of the islands had evolved a class-stratified society, with a caste, one characterized by the Spanish as nobles or chiefs, at the top. Their economies had developed into an intricate seaborne trade system that connected the islands.

Using a social structure somewhat similar to that of the Natchez and the Pacific Northwest Coast peoples, the Arawaks, whose culture centered in present-day Haiti (on the island of Hispaniola), were divided into three classes—the nobles, commoners (who paid tribute to the nobles), and servants, who often lived and worked in the nobles' homes. The island peoples had developed into sophisticated seafarers, traveling the open ocean in dugout canoes, some of which were large enough to carry about thirty men engaged in trade or peace missions. War, while known to the islanders, was rare among them.

Bartolomé de Las Casas, who arrived in the Indies in the early sixteenth century, pointed out later in his *History of the Indies* that the Spanish " . . . have so cruelly and inhumanely butchered [the Indians], that of three million people which

Hispaniola itself did contain, there are remaining alive scarce three hundred people. . . . [T]he islands of Cuba, . . . St. John, . . . Jamaica, and the Lucuyan Islands . . . are now totally unpeopled and destroyed; the inhabitants thereof amounting to above 500,000 souls. . . . [F]or . . . forty Years, wherein the Spanish exercised their abominable cruelties, and detestable tyrannies in those parts, . . . there have . . . perished above twelve million of souls, women and children being numbered in this sad and fatal list; moreover I do verily believe that I shall speak within compass, should I say that Fifty millions people were consumed in this Massacre."

While modern historians calculate that Hispaniola's original population was about 250,000 (not 3 million), Las Casas's testimony is nevertheless a searing tale of conquest and death for the Taino people. John Collier wrote that "according to Peschel, the ethnologist and historian, the population of Espanola [Hispaniola] in 1492 was less than 300,000 and more than 200,000. In 1508, the number of natives was 60,000; in 1510, 46,000; in 1512, 20,000; in 1514, 14,000. In 1548, it is doubtful if 500 natives of pure stock remained, and in 1570 only two villages of the Indians were left."

The Spanish conquest of the Aztecs (in Mexico) was aided by European diseases and, some historians feel, the Aztecs' own fear of a suddenly troubled future in the presence of Spanish conquistadores. The Spaniards' technology was superior but not by enough to swing the balance of power on its own. Hernán Cortés also began recruiting Indian allies against the Aztecs in the first city he visited on his way to Tenochtitlán, the Aztec capital. That city was Cempoalla, near the Gulf Coast, and housed about thirty thousand people of the Totonac Nation. The leaders of this city met Cortés on friendly terms and told him how intensely many of the Aztecs' tributary tribes hated them.

The Spanish soldier Bernal Díaz del Castillo described Tenochtitlán as one of the greatest cities in the world. While the solid temples, residences, and storehouses of the city gave it an air of permanence, the city was not old by Mesoamerican urban standards. Less than two centuries before Díaz saw it, the site had been little more than a small temple surrounded by a few mud-and-thatch huts. By 1519, however, Díaz found a city of unexpected splendor.

The famous Sunday market in the state of Oaxaca, Mexico, where Zapotec Indians sell produce and flowers in a colorful setting that subtly blends Spanish influences within the predominantly Native culture.

The Spanish kept a careful chronicle of this amazing new world. Friar Bernardino de Sahagún enlisted the aid of Aztec eyewitnesses and trained observers. Sahagún himself was fluent in Nahuatl, the Mexicas' language. While some Spanish conquistadores and priests warmed their hands over fires built from valuable artifacts and records that would have been of immense use to scholars today, the Franciscan friar Sahagún born in Spain in 1499, began a Franciscan school for the sons of surviving Aztec nobles. Sahagún prepared a massive twelve-part manuscript, the so-called *General History of the Things of New Spain*, treating all aspects of Aztec traditional lore. King Philip II of Spain refused to permit an edition of the work, and it was not published until 1830.

For decades to come, the Spanish conquest would extend further south into Mesoamerica (most of present-day Central America) and South America and north through Mexico and into huge portions of the present-day Southeast, West, and Southwest United States. In most cases, the Spanish conquest was marked by brutality and enslavement for Native people. But unlike the colonization of the Americas by other European groups, primarily the British, that established societies quite distinct and apart from those of the Natives whose lands they were settling, the Spanish colonization was marked by the intermingling of Native and European cultural and genetic strains. Much of this mixing of cultures was accomplished under the harsh yoke of forced servitude; much was accomplished by the persistent efforts of Spanish missionaries to convert Native people to Christianity. In the Southwest and Mexico, this "marriage" of Spanish and Native cultures is most evident in the ethnic and linguistic mix of the Pueblo and Mexican peoples.

In time, Spain would lose its colonial empire as various peoples in Central America and Mexico threw off Spanish rule, and many portions of New Spain that are now a part of the United States fell from Spanish control. By the time its holdings had shrunk, however, Spain, while no longer a political or military power in the Western Hemisphere, would have left a legacy of language and artistic, religious, and architectural influence that has made it a dominant cultural presence throughout the Americas.

— B. E. Johansen

SEE ALSO:

Arawak; Arizona; Aztec; California; Caribbean, Indigenous Cultures of; Catholic Church in the Spanish Empire; Central America, Indigenous Peoples of; Central and South Andean Culture Areas; Columbus, Christopher; Cortés, Hernán; Cuba; Doctrine of Discovery; Florida; Hispaniola; Jamaica; Las Casas, Bartolomé de; Latinos; Maya; Mexico, Indigenous People of; New Mexico; New Spain; Puerto Rico.

SUGGESTED READINGS:

Brandon, William. *The American Heritage Book of Indians*. New York: Dell, 1961.

Collier, John. *Indians of the Americas*. New York: New American Library, 1947.

Josephy, Alvin, ed. *America in 1492: The World of the Indian Peoples Before the Arrival of Columbus*. New York: Alfred A. Knopf, 1992.

Las Casas, Bartolomé de. *History of the Indies*, trans. and ed. by Andree Collard. New York: Harper & Row, 1971.

Stannard, David E. *American Holocaust: Columbus and the Conquest of the New World*. New York: Oxford University Press, 1992.

Thornton, Russell. *American Indian Holocaust and Survival: A Population History Since 1492*. Norman: University of Oklahoma Press, 1987.

Varner, John Greer, and Jeanette Johnson Varner. *Dogs of the Conquest*. Norman: University of Oklahoma Press, 1983.

SPEARFISHING

SEE Boldt, George Hugo; Bresette, Walter; Crabb, Barbara; Ecology, Native American Conceptions of; Fishing Rights; Lummi; Ojibwe; Washington State.

SPICER, EDWARD HOLLAND (1906–1983)

Edward Spicer, noted anthropologist, was born in Chittenham, Pennsylvania, in 1906. Spicer moved to Arizona in 1929 to facilitate his recovery from pulmonary tuberculosis. There he worked at a number of jobs before earning enough money to enroll at the University of Arizona. Spicer received his bachelor's degree in 1932 and his master's degree in anthropology in 1933. His master's thesis was based on archaeological fieldwork at King's Ruin, Arizona. He continued with archaeological work at Tuzigoot, Arizona, after receiving his degree, but in 1934, Spicer enrolled at the University of Chicago to study cultural anthropology. He received his Ph.D. in 1939 and returned to the University of Arizona as professor in 1946.

As a cultural anthropologist, Spicer was intrigued by the survival of traditional Native cultures in the American Southwest. This interest was first developed as he worked with Yaqui Indians in the 1930s while he was writing his dissertation and expanded to include other Native cultures in the Southwest and Mexico during the course of his career. His research led to the publication in 1962 of his most influential and original work, *Cycles of Conquest: The Impact of Spain, Mexico and the United States on the Indians of the Southwest, 1533–1960*. One of the basic themes of this work is that attempts by the dominant culture, whether it be Spanish, Mexican, or North American, to assimilate Native cultures in the Southwest have, for the most part, been failures. His ideas on the persistence of traditional cultures is further outlined in his book *The Yaquis: A Cultural History* (1980).

Spicer retired from teaching in 1978 and died in Tucson, Arizona, in 1983.

SEE ALSO:

Arizona; Mexico, Indigenous People of; New Mexico; New Spain; Spain; Yaqui.

SPIDER WOMAN

Spider Woman is an archetype, a symbol representing creation and protection. Also known as Grandmother Spider or Thought Woman, she appears in many Native American origin stories as a powerful creative deity. The Pawnee people know her as Red Spider Woman; she figures in their traditional telling of the origin of squash medicine. The Navajo people know Spider Woman as the creator who wove lightning, clouds, rainbows, and sunrays together on a giant loom to form the universe. She is credited with teaching people to weave. The Keres people know her as Thought Woman, who taught her sisters to sing life and medicine into being, while the Cherokee people attribute Grandmother Spider with bringing light to the earth. The Arapaho people have a name for the Supreme Being that may be translated as "spider."

Spider Woman is capable of creating something out of nothing by thinking it, singing it, or naming it. In many tales, she also intervenes in human affairs, protecting and guiding people and acting as a powerful transmitter of culture.

The Hopi people know Spider Woman as one of two initial beings: She represented the earth goddess and controlled the magic of the Below. Known as Kokyanwuhti, she and the sun god sang the earth into being. They created new beings with thought and song, and Spider Woman led them from the Underworld up through the sipapu (opening in the earth) to this world. It was with the guidance of Spider Woman that the Snake Dance was brought from the Underworld to the people above.

Spider Woman reappears in contemporary Native American literature. Author Paula Gunn Allen describes a spirit that pervades life—the spirit of the sacred female, a spirit of song, movement, and light. She tells us that there are many names for this spirit, called Spider Woman and Thought Woman. Spider Woman embodies the creative act as well as harmony and balance in the world. She represents the universal feminine principle of creation.

SEE ALSO:
Allen, Paula Gunn; Creation Stories; Snake Dance.

SPOTTED TAIL (1823–1881)

Spotted Tail (Sinte Galeshka) was a Brulé Sioux who became a major Sioux leader in the Plains Indian wars. He was born along the White River of South Dakota (or, as some accounts have it, near Laramie, Wyoming) to a mother named Walks with Pipe and a man named Cunka ("Tangled Hair"). Known as Jumping Buffalo in his youth, Spotted Tail got his adult name from a striped raccoon pelt given him by a trapper.

Known as an extremely valiant man, Spotted Tail won his laurels as a chief by his skills in battle and diplomacy; his title was not hereditary. On one occasion in about 1855, Spotted Tail and two other men gave themselves up at Fort Laramie to spare the rest of the tribe after an unidentified Brulé was charged with murder. During his imprisonment for a crime he did not commit, Spotted Tail learned to read and write English.

During the early 1860s, after his release, the tribal council ignored the hereditary line and selected Spotted Tail when Chief Little Thunder died. Spotted Tail refused to sign a treaty in 1865, but later he did sign the 1868 Fort Laramie Treaty, which was to have assured Native rights to the Black Hills. In 1871, Spotted Tail served on a buffalo hunt as guide to the grand duke Alexis of Russia.

In 1875, Spotted Tail was among the Lakota chiefs who traveled to Washington, D.C., to negotiate the sale of the Black Hills. Spotted Tail played a central role in negotiations with government officials in which all offers to buy the Black Hills were refused. But it was too late. By the time Spotted Tail spoke, more than ten thousand miners had swarmed into the hills, seeking the gold that George Armstrong Custer's 1874 expedition had found there.

Spotted Tail was an unusually strong-willed administrator; he maintained a police force to keep whiskey merchants off the reservation, and he deplored threats by the army to relocate the Lakota to Indian Territory (now Oklahoma). Spotted Tail forbade young warriors to raid non-Indian settlements, and when a European-American man was murdered, he turned the perpetrator over to Euro-American authorities—then hired a lawyer to represent the man and paid for it out of his own pocket.

Throughout the 1870s, Spotted Tail was accused by Red Cloud of pocketing the proceeds from a sale of tribal land. Possibly as a result of this dispute, Spotted Tail was shot to death by Crow Dog, a Sioux subchief, on August 5, 1881.

SEE ALSO:
Black Hills; Crow Dog; Custer, George Armstrong; Fort Laramie Treaty of 1868; Oklahoma; Red Cloud; Siouan Nations; Wars, Indian.

A group of prominent Sioux leaders poses with Julius Meyer, who is probably their attorney or interpreter, in an undated photo from the 1800s. From left to right they are Sitting Bull, Meyer, Swift Bear, Red Cloud, and Spotted Tail.

SQUANTO (c. 1580–1622)

A Wampanoag, Squanto (Tisquantum) was one of the first Indians to aid English colonists. Kidnapped from his native land in 1614 by English explorers, he was sold along with twenty Patuxet companions on the slave market at Málaga, Spain. A Christian friar smuggled Squanto to England, where he worked for a rich merchant as he learned the English language. Squanto obtained passage back to North America on a trading ship, before the arrival of the Pilgrims, who came ashore in 1620.

Squanto surprised the Pilgrims by greeting them in English, as he and other Native Americans helped the new immigrants survive their first American winter. When the seeds of English wheat, barley and peas did not grow, Squanto showed the immigrants how to plant corn in hillocks, using dead herring as fertilizer. Squanto also taught them how to design traps to catch fish; in addition, he acted as a guide and interpreter.

Squanto was acting as an emissary of Massasoit, head chief of the Wampanoags, who had decided to aid the Pilgrims after their landing in North America. (During the next fifty years, the number of immigrants increased to the point where the last of the Wampanoags' land was threatened. At that point, Metacom—known to the English as King Philip—a son of Massasoit, rose to a position of leadership in 1676 in what became known as King Philip's War, the last rebellion of Native peoples in New England.)

In 1622, Squanto died of smallpox, which had been brought into his community by European settlers.

SEE ALSO:
King Philip's War; Massasoit; Narragansett; Wampanoag.

Squanto is portrayed in a pose that typifies his place in most histories of early colonial America: capably, maybe even a bit heroically, helping an English settler.

SQUAXIN ISLAND

The Squaxin Island Reservation is located in Mason County, Washington State, with its tribal headquarters in Shelton, Washington. The tribe has an enrolled membership of 374 individuals, with 127 living on-reservation. The Squaxin Island Reservation contains 2,175 acres (881 hectares) and was established by the Medicine Creek Treaty in 1854. The Squaxin Island Tribe accepted the 1934 Indian Reorganization Act (also known as the Indian New Deal). In 1965, the tribe approved a tribal constitution that established a five-member tribal council, elected to serve three-year terms. The Squaxin Island Tribe has treaty fishing rights and is a member of the Northwest Indian Fisheries Commission.

SEE ALSO:

Indian New Deal (Indian Reorganization Act of 1934); Washington Coast and Puget Sound Indians, History of.

STANDING BEAR, LUTHER
(1868–1939)

An Oglala Lakota, Luther Standing Bear was one of the founders of a remarkable Sioux literary tradition that includes Charles Eastman, Gertrude Bonnin, and Vine Deloria, Jr. Recognition of Standing Bear's works, which range from social commentary to autobiography, grew toward the end of the twentieth century. His work encourages a pan-Indian sense of identity.

Standing Bear was at first called Ota Kre ("Plenty Kill") because of his father's reputation as a warrior. The young Standing Bear was trained traditionally—to become a hunter and warrior— just as the increasing European-American presence was making the old ways impossible. He was a member of the first class to attend the Carlisle Indian School in Pennsylvania. Later, Standing Bear recounted how the young students were lined up in front of a blackboard with symbols on it that they didn't understand. Each was told to choose a "white man's name." Standing Bear chose "Luther."

As a young man on leave from Carlisle Indian School, Standing Bear attended a speech in 1884 in Philadelphia given by the legendary Hunkpapa Sioux Chief Sitting Bull, who stressed the need for education and reported that he was about to talk peace with the Great Father in Washington. The white "translator" told the audience that Sitting Bull was recounting the Battle of the Little Bighorn in lurid detail. "He [the translator] told so many lies that I had to smile," Standing Bear wrote later.

Standing Bear's father had participated in the Custer fight and later represented his people at a conference in Washington, D.C. Standing Bear's father returned from that conference dressed in a Prince Albert coat and other formal trappings, including a silk top hat that was later used to carry water.

During his own life, Standing Bear was not as well known as Eastman or Bonnin. He often survived from job to job, working with Buffalo Bill's Wild West show for a time. Standing Bear was an unabashed Native traditionalist during a time when the dominant culture's attitude was "kill the Indian, save the man," the slogan invented by General R. H. Pratt, founder of Carlisle Indian School, to describe assimilation.

Standing Bear turned to writing late in his life and wrote four books intended to describe his people. The first was *My People, the Sioux* (1928), a memoir that described the debate over allotment among the Lakotas. In 1931, Standing Bear published an autobiographical work, *My Indian Boyhood*, followed by *Land of the Spotted Eagle* (1933) and *Stories of the Sioux* (1934).

In 1933, Standing Bear wrote to President Franklin Roosevelt suggesting that a bill be drawn up to require the teaching of American Indian history and culture in non-Indian schools. This idea foreshadowed the establishment of Native American studies programs around the United States after 1970.

Standing Bear also played leading roles in several motion pictures, beginning with *White Oak* (1921) and including *Santa Fe Trail* (1930). He died while he was working on the film *Union Pacific* in 1939.

SEE ALSO:

Bonnin, Gertrude; Buffalo Bill Cody; Carlisle Indian School; Deloria, Vine, Jr.; Eastman, Charles; Little Bighorn, Battle of the; Sitting Bull.

STOMP DANCING

Stomp Dancing is a religious practice of the tribes of the U.S. Southeast, primarily the Creeks, Seminoles, Cherokees, Chickasaws, and Choctaws, although other tribes have borrowed this dance as well. Stomp Dancing is sometimes performed for social reasons as well as religious purposes; in such cases, the dances will be held outside the ceremonial grounds, called Stomp Grounds. The Seminoles and Creeks have the most Stomp Ground land in Oklahoma. Unlike the daytime dances at the Green Corn Ceremony (held in conjunction with the corn harvest), which is the highlight of the religious calendar in many Southeast tribes, Stomp Dancing occurs at night. Dances take place at monthly intervals beginning in the spring and ending in the fall, and during Green Corn, there are nights of dancing on each of the three evenings of this religious ceremony.

When the dances are performed in their religious context, they take place in the center of the grounds between four arbors. In the early evening, the chief's speaker goes around and cries out at half-hour intervals that an evening of dancing is about to start. To begin the dances, the leader enters the square ground with his assistants and begins to walk around the sacred fire. Other men who can answer the songs fall in behind them, coming from the edges of the square or from where they are seated in an arbor. After a sufficient number of men have fallen in, women follow and walk slowly around the fire. The leader sings several phrases that the men echo and eventually begins the stomp step; the other dancers follow. Women provide the rhythm of the dance by shaking turtle shells attached to their feet through a skillful toe-heel action, creating a beat that sounds something like *shuguta shuguta shuguta*. The male leader continues singing out phrases that the dancers behind him echo, and he leads them in concentric circles around the fire in the center of the square. The leader may stop and dance in place, waving his arms up and down while facing the fire, honoring the fire that, in southeastern storytelling, is the embodiment of the sun.

A sequence of different songs continues all night long until the morning. The compelling sound of the women's turtle shells rattling and the men singing out under the arbors on an Oklahoma summer night creates a powerful impression. There is not an official outfit for Stomp Dancing, though many participants wear Seminole-style skirts and blouses if they are women, and cowboy hats with attached feathers if they are men. The men might also wear a yarn sash with large tassels on the end or a Seminole-style vest.

Readers need to be cautious when encountering older texts describing Stomp Dancing. Some racist historians and ethnographers have described the dances as "drunken orgies" and assumed they have no contemporary meaning. This is patently untrue; anyone entering the grounds while drunk is quickly ushered out because it is believed that such disrespect can weaken the medicine (the spiritual power of the dance) or even cause harm to the participants. In earlier times, light horsemen, an Oklahoma Creek police force, would severely punish anyone showing up at the ceremonial grounds drunk; sometimes the offenders would be tied to a tree and whipped. The punishment was harsh, but the welfare of the community at large was at stake because disrespect at the ceremonial grounds had consequences in the spiritual world.

Willie Lena's book *Oklahoma Seminoles: Medicine, Magic, and Religion*, published by the University of Oklahoma Press, provides a full account of the Stomp Dance and the Green Corn Ceremony.

SEE ALSO:

Cherokee; Chickasaw; Choctaw; Creek; Green Corn Ceremony; Seminole.

STONEY INDIAN

SEE Assiniboine.

STORYTELLING

Native Americans, like other peoples, produce a wide variety of literature in a variety of forms. One of the most enduring narrative forms for American Indians is storytelling. Storytelling has been and continues to be an oral art form, but since European contact, Native Americans have also become skillful at telling stories in print, producing a number of talented and nationally recognized novelists, poets, essayists, and autobiographers.

Traditional oral literature comes in many forms, including stories, songs, poems, and chants, with a wide range of audiences and purposes. A chant, for instance, such as the Cherokee going-to-water

Members of the Dawnland Singers, a group of Abenaki musicians from New York State, use storytelling and other elements of the oral tradition, including a type of call-and-response interplay with the audience, in their performances.

formula, is said at dawn next to running water in order to ensure the Cherokee family long life. A story might describe the origins of the tribe and its ceremonies—like the Creek migration account when the people emerge from below the earth out onto the broader landscape and journey toward the origin of the sun, eventually settling along the Chattahoochee River. A story might be about a tribal trickster, like the Kiowa stories of Saynday. These stories begin with "Saynday was on the path" or "Saynday was going along" and describe Saynday's journeys, his tricks that sometimes backfire, and his power as someone who brings many useful things to Kiowa people, as well as the trouble he often gets people into. A story might involve a cultural hero, like the Iroquois hero Ragged Boy, who comes across the Little People and helps them. In exchange, they give Ragged Boy strawberries, which he takes back to his people, who are in the midst of a famine, establishing a reciprocal relationship between the Little People and the Iroquois.

Or a story could be about a historical event that Native people remember and tell. Some Oklahoma Indians who follow the oral tradition still recall the events of Indian Removal in the 1830s when, in some tribes, half the population was lost on the removal trails. Many Lakotas have relatives who were massacred by the U.S. Cavalry at Wounded Knee in 1890, and they pass these events on in the form of stories.

Native American people still tell stories and are continually updating the oral tradition. Stories can be entertaining; stories can be medicine (a form of spiritual empowerment); stories can be a form of protest or witness; stories can be many things.

Through oral storytelling, events are reexperienced. In an oral culture, word and deed are closely associated. In comparison, in writing systems, a word is a symbol, and the human mind converts the letters into sounds. In an oral culture, the spoken word is, by definition, an action, not a symbol. Spoken words require sound and motion, movement in one's body, the vibration of vocal cords, the expulsion of air. In an oral culture, people think differently and see the world differently than in a written culture because words become associated with actions. Words can make things happen; words expend physical forces upon the universe. Even as it is being told, a story becomes a reliving of events.

When oral communities need to pass on information, it is often done in the form of stories. The elders, who have over the years had the opportunity to hear the most stories, become the encyclopedias, the reference works, the books of the culture. In the absence of writing, it is easier to remember stories with action, characters, and dialogue than it is to remember abstract statements about how things should be. Consequently, much information is placed within a story so that it will be remembered and passed on.

This is not to say that oral communities are incapable of abstraction and analysis, though some scholars of oral theory have argued that trying to analyze a story would break the storytelling spell, so that the listener would forget the story and be unable to pass it on. In oral cultures, stories are sometimes reinforced with music, dance, body movements, gestures, and voice changes, and these scholars claim that this demands a total physical and emotional involvement with the story that does not leave the listener time to think about the story or analyze it. However, it is human nature to think about what one has heard after hearing it; the assumption that no one would make connections between stories assumes a world without curiosity and questioning.

Many contemporary Native writers borrow from the oral tradition, taking the old stories and recasting them in light of modern events, making them relevant to the lives of Indian people today. A good example is Louise Erdrich's masterwork, the novel *Love Medicine*. The character Lipsha is on a search to determine his parentage; by the end of the story, he finds out the truth about his mother, June, and ends up on a journey toward the Canadian border with his father, Gerry Nanapush. In traditional Ojibwe (Chippewa) storytelling, Nanabush is a trickster figure of tremendous height and stature, capable of changing shapes and making incredible escapes. Gerry, the character in

Love Medicine whose name resembles that of Nanabush, is able to elude the law and slip out of tight corners by means that are extraordinary, if not supernatural. One of the Nanabush stories from Ojibwe tradition tells of Nanabush setting out in search for his father, and this is paralleled in *Love Medicine* by Lipsha's encounter with his father, Gerry, who has escaped from the federal penitentiary. There is not a perfect one-to-one correspondence between the Nanabush stories and *Love Medicine*; nonetheless, the similarity demonstrates the way in which Native authors apply the oral tradition to contemporary writing. In this way, storytelling continues in a format that contemporary people can have access to. This is not to say that oral storytelling is the same thing as written literature, but the two forms of storytelling complement each other, and both continue to be important.

— C. S. Womack

SEE ALSO:

Coyote Stories; Creation Stories; Erdrich, Louise; Oral History; Removal Act, Indian; Tricksters; Wounded Knee (1890).

SUGGESTED READINGS:

Brumble, David H. *American Indian Autobiography*. Berkeley: University of California Press, 1988.

Krupat, Arnold. *For Those Who Come After: A Study of Native American Autobiography*. Berkeley: University of California Press, 1985.

Momaday, N. Scott. *The Way to Rainy Mountain*. Albuquerque: University of New Mexico Press, 1969.

Oliver, Louis Littlecoon. *Chasers of the Sun: Creek Indian Thoughts*. Greenfield, NY: Greenfield Review Press, 1990.

Sarris, Greg. *Keeping Slug Woman Alive: A Holistic Approach to American Indian Texts*. Berkeley: University of California Press, 1993.

Scarberry-Garcia, Susan. *Landmarks of Healing: A Study of House Made of Dawn*. Albuquerque: University of New Mexico Press, 1990.

Swann, Brian. *On the Translation of Native American Literatures*. Washington, DC: Smithsonian Institution Press, 1992.

———. *Smoothing the Ground: Essays on Native American Oral Literature*. Berkeley: University of California Press, 1983.

Walters, Anna Lee. *Talking Indian: Reflections on Survival and Writing.* New York: Firebrand Books, 1992.

STUDI, WES (c. 1946–)

Born Wesley Studie in Nofire Hollow, Oklahoma, this contemporary actor is the eldest son of a ranch hand and a housekeeper. Studi's first language is Cherokee, and he didn't learn English until he started school.

Studi attended an Indian boarding school in Chilocco, Oklahoma. Upon graduation, he was drafted into the army and sent to Vietnam for a tour of duty in 1967. Studi enrolled at Tulsa Junior College after returning to the United States, then joined the Trail of Broken Treaties protest march (1972), during which he briefly occupied the Bureau of Indian Affairs (BIA) building in Washington, D.C. The following year, he joined the protest at Wounded Knee, South Dakota, and was arrested for insurrection, jailed, and released on condition he leave the state.

Studi worked next as a reporter for the *Tulsa Indian News*, and in 1974 married his second wife, Rebecca Graves, a Cherokee schoolteacher. They lived on a horse ranch near Tulsa with their son and daughter until their divorce in 1982. In 1983, Studi joined the American Indian Theater Company in Tulsa. He made his film debut in *Powwow Highway* (1988) and married singer Maura Dhu soon after that. As a struggling actor, Studi appeared in some commercials and had a small role as a Pawnee warrior, The Toughest, in *Dances with Wolves* (1990). His breakthrough role, however, was that of the angry and vengeful Magua in *The Last of the Mohicans* (1992). Studi was electrifying in the role, drawing on his own anger and bitterness about the history of the Cherokee Nation. In addition to his film credits, Studi has worked in several television projects, including "The Broken Chain" (an episode in Turner Broadcasting System's 1993 series *The Native Americans)*, and the made-for-TV movie of Larry McMurtry's *Streets of Laredo* (1995).

Studi's first leading role was that of Geronimo in the motion picture *Geronimo: An American Legend* (1994). Aware of the importance of his por-

trayal of Geronimo, whom he considers a symbol of resistance, Studi worked hard researching the role and studying the Apache language. Although the film was not well reviewed, Studi has established himself as a contemporary actor of note, and he looks forward to playing different kinds of roles in the future—roles that are not culturally specific to his Native background.

SEE ALSO:

Boarding Schools; Cherokee; Geronimo; Hollywood, Indians, and Indian Images; Trail of Broken Treaties; Wounded Knee, Confrontation at (1973).

SUQUAMISH TRIBE OF THE PORT MADISON RESERVATION

The Suquamish Port Madison Reservation is located in Kitsap County in Washington State, with its tribal headquarters in Suquamish, Washington. The tribe has 760 enrolled members, with 388 living on-reservation. The reservation contains 7,285 acres (2,950 hectares) and was established in 1855 by the Point Elliott Treaty. The reservation was enlarged by executive order in 1864.

The Suquamish Nation contains members of three tribes: Suquamish, Duwamish, and Muckleshoot. The tribe approved a constitution in 1965 and created a seven-member council to oversee tribal assets, programs, and businesses, including a tribal salmon hatchery. Each council member serves a three-year term. The Suquamish have treaty fishing rights and are a member of the Northwest Indian Fisheries Commission.

SEE ALSO:

Washington Coast and Puget Sound Indians, History of.

TAINO

The Tainos are Arawakan Indian people who inhabited various Caribbean islands until the mid-1600s. These island Arawakans originally migrated to the Caribbean from tropical South American rain forests in the fourteenth or fifteenth century. Calling themselves the Taino, they settled in the Bahamas, Greater Antilles, and Trinidad, where they quickly established a highly developed and politically organized culture based on agriculture, fishing, and hunting sea mammals.

The Tainos brought with them a sophisticated system of raising root plants called *conuco*. After burning fertile forest areas and forming mounds out of the rich ash, they planted bitter yucca, yams, peanuts, and other root plants, as well as peppers, corn, beans, tobacco, squash, and even pineapple. Once planted, these crops required little tending. Fishing and hunting supplied protein in the form of iguanas and other reptiles; pigeons and parrots; shellfish, fish, and turtles; snakes; and sea mammals such as the manatee or sea cow.

The Tainos have been described as peaceful, gentle, friendly, and ceremonious, rarely involved in warfare, except when provoked by their aggressive Carib neighbors. The Caribs, who had also migrated from the Amazon basin, drove the Tainos out of the Lesser Antilles when they first tried to settle there, and then continued to raid other Taino settlements, often killing the men and taking the women and children as slaves.

Taino communities typically consisted of many multifamily households that held as many as fifty people each. Each household was governed by a headman, usually the most able-bodied male. Villages were governed by either one of these headmen or a group of them. Each island was ruled by a chief, and larger islands were often subdivided into several provinces ruled by subchiefs.

Because of the temperate climate, the Tainos did not have to build elaborate housing or spend a lot of time gathering food. This left them with the leisure time to design and produce superbly crafted pottery, baskets, woven cotton cloth, and elaborate stone sculptures. Both men and women enjoyed decorating their bodies with paint and with jewelry of gold, stone, bone, and shell. They brewed several kinds of fermented drinks and smoked tobacco. They also enjoyed ball games, feasts, and dances.

Taino religious systems were also highly organized, presided over by priests or holy men who claimed the ability to capture good and evil spirits inside statues they called *zemis*. The Tainos also believed their holy men could cure illness, protect hunters and warriors from harm, and see into the future. Holy men also presided over the elaborate death rituals and other religious ceremonies.

In spite of ongoing attacks from neighboring Caribs, Taino culture thrived until the Spanish arrived in the mid-1500s. Spanish settlers needed laborers for their plantations and gold mines and immediately set out to capture Taino men, women, and children for this purpose. Some of the Tainos tried to rebel; more fled to the hills, other islands, or back to the South American mainland, but few of those who resisted survived. Those not killed outright died as Spanish slaves or from the epidemic diseases the Spanish brought with them from Europe. Although people of Taino ancestry still live in and around the Caribbean, the Taino culture was largely decimated by the waves of newcomers from Europe.

SEE ALSO:
Arawak; Bahamas; Caribbean, Indigenous Cultures of; Columbus, Christopher; Cuba; Puerto Rico.

TALLCHIEF, MARIA (1925–)

Osage ballerina Maria Tallchief has achieved international distinction with ballet companies in both Europe and North America. She was born in the Osage Nation, in Oklahoma, in 1925. By the age of four, she was studying ballet and music. When she was eight, her family moved to California, where she continued to study ballet in the Los Angeles area under some of the world's best-known ballet teachers, including Bronislava Nijinska, David Lichine, and George Balanchine. She danced her first solo performance at the Hollywood Bowl when she was fifteen years old.

She then joined the famous Ballet Russe, a Russian ballet troupe. When her former teacher, George Balanchine, became head of the troupe, her career began to soar. In 1942, she married Balanchine, a marriage that would last for ten years. They moved to Paris, where she became the first American ballerina to dance with the Paris Opera Ballet. Upon returning to the United States, she quickly established herself as the prima ballerina in the Balanchine Ballet Society, which later became the New York City Ballet. Her most noted role was her performance of Balanchine's *Firebird*. She continued to perform full-time until 1959, when she formed her own dance troupe. She retired from dancing in 1966. In 1974, she developed a dance troupe to perform with the Chicago Lyric Opera, and until 1979, she also directed the Opera Ballet School in Chicago.

In addition to being a legendary ballerina, Tallchief is also recognized as a great teacher of ballet. While working with dancers in Chicago, she was able to teach others the very difficult leading role that she danced in *Firebird*.

TAMANEND

Tamanend (often called Tammany by non-Natives), a Lenape (Delaware) chief friendly to William Penn, became a popular figure in the folklore of early Pennsylvania. Although the real Tamanend's mark appeared on only two treaties (June 23, 1683, and June 15, 1692), he was destined to become a legendary figure in United States and Pennsylvania history and folklore.

Tradition has it that Tamanend's name meant "The Affable" and that he was one of the Lenape Indians who welcomed William Penn on his arrival in North America on October 27, 1682. By July 6, 1694, in a meeting between the provincial council of Pennsylvania and a delegation of Indians, he had become a strong supporter of the Europeans and their policies. From these facts and folklore, a legendary Tamanend was constructed in the early eighteenth century who was the white man's friend and counselor.

Osage ballerina Maria Tallchief in costume for *The Dying Swan,* which she danced with the New York City Ballet.

Eventually, the celebration of Tamanend's friendship was fused with British May Day traditions. Once this fusion took place, the peace, justice, freedom, and strength characteristic of American Indian confederacies became a beacon to some of the American revolutionaries who sought an alternative to the unlimited power of the British monarchy. As early as 1637, American Indians and colonists erected maypoles—usually pine trees made into posts about eighty feet (twenty-four meters) high—for revelry and celebration on May Day. Often, the colonists nailed buck horns near the top of the posts and invited American Indians to the celebrations. In this way, the English rite of spring became "Americanized" with American Indian participation.

Building upon the popularity of such early celebrations, Chief Tamanend's mythic importance among the people of Philadelphia crystalized when a group of Quakers established the Schuylkill Fishing Company in 1732. Claiming that their fishing rights in the Schuylkill River had been given to them by this Lenape chief and friend to William Penn, the company adopted him as its patron saint. The saint's day was designated as May 1, the traditional beginning of the fishing season. At this time, Chief Tamanend was viewed by many Philadelphians as a nature spirit whose ritual day was celebrated to assure a bountiful fishing season, but he seems to also have been associated with a resolve to protect the fishing rights (and by proxy, the political rights) of its members.

Within a decade, the Schuylkill Fishing Company began to fictionalize Tamanend by creating mottos attributed to him. In 1747, the company gave a cannon to the Association Battery of Philadelphia, stamped *Kwanio Che Keeteru* ("This is my right, and I will defend it"), a phrase attributed to Tamanend. The phrase was ripe with implications for the increasingly restless colonists. By the time of the Stamp Act crisis eighteen years later, images of the Indian were being used widely as a symbol of resistance to British authority.

Over time, Tamanend's name, appropriated often by non-Indians, was corrupted to "Tammany." The most scandalous use of "Tammany" was as the title of the corrupt society that dominated New York City politics in the nineteenth century, whose executive committee was known as Tammany Hall. As "Tammany," however, the chief's name was used before this.

Tammany had been transformed into a powerful mythic figure that would help to mold the new nation's identity. On May 1, 1771, an account of a Tammany Day celebration described people who entered a room, singing songs, "giving the whoop, and dancing in the style of those people" (i.e., American Indians).

SEE ALSO:
American Revolution; Penn, William; Tammany Society.

TAMMANY SOCIETY

Many colonial Americans viewed American society as a synthesis of Native American and European cultures. The Tammany Society, a classic example of the blending of the two cultures, was a broad-based popular movement that encouraged the use of symbols and beliefs indigenous to North America in the founding of the United States. It also appropriated the name of a Lenape (Delaware) chief, Tamanend, and changed it to "Tammany." The Tammany Society espoused a philosophy that colonial America was a unique synthesis of the best and noblest aspects of Europe and America—Native America, that is. The celebration of Tammany Day may also have been an attempt to adapt May Day and other "Old World" holidays to the new American environment.

On May 1, 1777, John Adams enthusiastically reported the origin of St. Tammany Day in Philadelphia to his wife, Abigail: "This is King Tammany's Day. Tammany was an Indian King, of this part of the Continent, when Mr. Penn first came here. His court was in this town. He was friendly to Mr. Penn and very serviceable to him. He lived here among the first settlers for some time and until old age."

Building upon their own experiences with Indians, founders of the United States such as James Madison and Thomas Jefferson used the Tammany Society and its membership to forge a new democratic party. Other founding fathers, such as Benjamin Franklin, John Dickinson, and Benjamin Rush, became influential members of the society.

On May 1, 1772, the Sons of King Tammany met in Philadelphia as the successor to the Sons of Liberty, an organization that promoted the separation of the colonies from the monarchy and used disruptive tactics to stir rebellion against the British. The Tammany Society toasted themselves, "St. George, St. Andrew, St. Patrick, and St. David." They also proclaimed that all the saints (including the American Indian Tammany) should "love each other as the brethren of one common ancestor." Furthermore, the Tammany Society believed that all the ethnic societies should unite "in their hearty endeavors to preserve their native Constitutional American Liberties." By 1773, the society in Philadelphia had grown disenchanted with King George III, so its members performed a mock "canonization" of King Tammany. With this mock canonization, the organization fused a folk holiday (May Day) with a patriotic organization. Very soon, Tammany Societies began to appear in other colonies.

Shortly after Adams described the Tammany Society in 1777, the Oneidas brought corn to the starving Revolutionary Army at Valley Forge and ensured their survival as a fighting force. The men of the Continental Army did not forget this debt; on May 1, 1778, with the bitter winter over, the Continental Army at Valley Forge held a Tammany Day celebration.

By the end of the Revolution, the Tammany Society in Philadelphia was known as the "Constitutional Sons of St. Tammany." As early as 1772, the Philadelphia Tammany Society dedicated itself to the preservation of their "native Constitutional American Liberties." The Tammany Society was a potent political force by the 1780s, and its members delighted in welcoming Indian delegations to the cities of Philadelphia and New York.

Following the Revolution, chapters of the Tammany Society quickly spread throughout the states and the Northwest Territory. Traditional May Day celebrations in the name of St. Tammany were celebrated from Georgia to Rhode Island and on the banks of the Ohio River. In many cases, the postrevolutionary Tammany societies were outgrowths of the local Sons of Liberty. This was especially true of the New York and Philadelphia branches of the society.

Tammany Society rituals were often marked with parades and other public observances. During April of 1786, the Tammany Society welcomed Chief Cornplanter and five other Senecas to Philadelphia. In a remarkable ceremony, the Tammany sachems escorted the Senecas from their lodgings at the Indian Queen tavern to Tammany's wigwam on the banks of the Schuylkill River for a conference.

In Philadelphia on May 1, 1786, St. Tammany's Day was marked with the usual celebrations and feasts, after which a portrait of Cornplanter was given to the Tammany Society. After the toasts were finished, the Tammany sachems and a great number of spectators proceeded to the residence of "brother Benjamin Franklin who appearing was saluted," and Franklin thanked them for the "honour paid him, then the brothers all retired to their own wigwams." In May of 1786, celebrations were noted as far away as Savannah, Georgia, and Richmond, Virginia. The last toast in Richmond stated, "May the great spirit encircle the whole world in the belt of friendship."

The image of Saint Tammany long outlived its prerevolutionary roots. Tammany was the main character in a 1795 Broadway play and reappeared as "Tamenund" at the conclusion of James Fenimore Cooper's *Last of the Mohicans*. Tammany, like the Tea Party Mohawks, was used to express a distinct American identity in the face of Europe, as well as to agitate for popular rule. The rhetoric of the Tammany Society illustrates how deftly the Native character of America had become interwoven with that of the immigrants' self-image by the beginning of the nineteenth century.

— B. E. Johansen

SEE ALSO:
Cornplanter; Franklin, Benjamin; Penn, William; Revere, Paul; Tamanend.

TAOS BLUE LAKE ACT

SEE Blue Lake; Taos Pueblo.

TAOS PUEBLO

Taos Pueblo is a Tiwa-speaking pueblo located seventy miles (113 kilometers) north of Santa Fe, New Mexico, along a small stream named Rio Pueblo de Taos. In 1910, Taos Pueblo had a population of 515. In 1991, the population was 1,601, with another 500 enrolled members of the pueblo living elsewhere. The pueblo is located about three miles (five kilometers) from the New Mexico town of Taos, which is a popular resort noted for its many art galleries. Taos Pueblo itself receives more than one million tourist visitors each year, making tourism one of its principal economic activities.

The pueblo is one of the few pueblos in New Mexico to remain in its original location since the beginning of Spanish colonization in 1598. The pueblo was constructed more than six hundred years ago, probably sometime around the year 1350. No

An old Spanish mission and cemetery at Taos Pueblo, New Mexico.

Taos Pueblo potter Virginia Romero. Located just outside the city of Taos, New Mexico—now a popular haven for artists and craftspeople—Taos Pueblo draws over one million tourists a year.

electricity or running water is allowed inside the old pueblo, and ladders are still used to reach the upper floors. Today, the Taos reservation encompasses about 95,000 acres (38,475 hectares).

The pueblo sits at the foot of Taos Mountain, which is sacred to the people of the pueblo. Especially revered is Blue Lake near the summit, to which the village makes an annual migration and conducts a ceremony each August. In 1906, Blue Lake and 48,000 acres (19,440 hectares) of surrounding land were taken from the pueblo by the United States government and incorporated into the Carson National Forest. The people of the pueblo began a long court battle with the government to have their sacred land restored to them, finally achieving success in 1970. Their victory marked the first time that Indians had succeeded in having land restored to them, rather than being offered monetary compensation for losses.

Taos Pueblo has no clan system. In its place, a strong extended family kinship system maintains strong loyalty to the community. The governmental system is also a very old one, one that places most of the power in a large council of elders, which consists of about sixty men. Leadership positions are held for only one-year periods. The continuity of its form of government is recognized as one of the factors in making the pueblo one of the most successful in maintaining its traditions, its worldview, and its sense of community.

Historically, the people of Taos Pueblo have been agriculturalists and hunters, with livestock providing a secondary economic activity. Today, the people are participating more in the economy of the United States, with many of them pursuing full-time employment and others seeking higher education. Regardless of economic changes, the traditions and culture of the pueblo remain strong.

A pair of ovens stand outside a home at Taos Pueblo, New Mexico. The pueblo is remarkable for having preserved much of its traditional style.

The pueblo and the nearby town of Taos played a significant role during the fur-trapping era of the early nineteenth century. In the early twentieth century, the area became attractive to authors, and a writers' colony thrived in the area. In more recent years, artists have found the area an attractive place to live. Throughout all the many changes in the region, the pueblo has remained very much the same as it was during the Spanish colonial era. Taos Pueblo is known throughout the world and was recently nominated as a World Heritage site.

SEE ALSO:
Blue Lake; New Mexico; New Spain; Pueblo; Tiwa Pueblos; Tourism.

TEACHING STORIES

SEE Storytelling; Tricksters.

TEBBEL, JOHN WILLIAM (1912–)

John William Tebbel may be the most prolific of all writers of Indian descent. Tebbel was born in Boyle City, Michigan, in 1912 and is of Ojibwe (Chippewa) ancestry. According to Tebbel, his great-grandmother was known as Woman of the Green Glade and keeper of the oral tradition of the Ojibwe tribe. He received his B.A. degree from Central Michigan University and an M.S. degree from Columbia University.

During his long career as a journalist and free-lance writer, Tebbel worked for such publications as the *Detroit Free Press*, the *American Mercury*, *Newsweek*, and the *New York Times* and has served as associate editor for E. P. Dutton & Company (a publishing house) and as a professor of journalism and head of the journalism department at New York University. From 1958 to 1962, Tebbel directed the Graduate Institute of Book Publishing at New York University. He has also served as a consultant to the Ford Foundation. In addition to three historical novels, Tebbel has also published a large number of nonfiction books and more than five hundred articles in popular magazines.

John Tebbel's first historical novel was *The Conqueror*, which was published in 1951. It is based on the life of Sir William Johnson, British superintendent-general of Indian affairs in North America in the years before the French and Indian War. The novel traces Johnson's role as the spokesperson for the Iroquois Confederacy.

Tebbel's second historical novel, *Touched with Fire*, was published in 1952 and is the story of the life of Sieur de La Salle (also known as Robert Cavelier, the French explorer) and his adventures from the Mississippi River to the Canadian tundra. A *Voice in the Streets*, Tebbel's third historical novel, published in 1954, is set in New York City during the 1800s and is the story of one Irish immigrant's rise from poverty to wealth and power. Among Tebbel's many nonfiction works are two books on the American Indian Wars.

A 1954 publicity photo of Ojibwe writer John Tebbel.

SEE ALSO:
French and Indian War; Iroquois Confederacy; Johnson, William; Wars, Indian.

TECUMSEH

Tecumseh was a Shawnee leader who appealed to Indians of all Eastern Woodlands tribes to form a confederacy to oppose U.S. westward expansion in the early nineteenth century. In this effort, he was initially greatly aided by his younger brother, Tenskwatawa, who became known as the Shawnee Prophet. Tenskwatawa attracted a large number of people with his preaching for a return to traditional Indian ways and the rejection of European ideas and products.

Tecumseh was born in present-day western Ohio in 1768. His grandfather had served as principal war chief of the Shawnee Nation, and his father held that position at the time Tecumseh was born. Much is known about Tecumseh's personal life, including his family members. His father, Pucksinwah, was killed while Tecumseh was still a boy. Tecumseh's upbringing and training was then assumed by his older brother, Chicksika. As a young warrior, Tecumseh followed Chicksika on many excursions, until Chicksika was killed in Tennessee, by which time Tecumseh had become a leader himself.

Tecumseh's mother is thought to have been either Cherokee or Creek. When Tecumseh was eleven years old, his mother, Methoataske, moved to southeastern Missouri with nearly one thousand Shawnees who did not wish to remain in

Shawnee leader Tecumseh, whose wish to halt U.S. expansion into the West led him to attempt to form a vast confederacy of eastern Indian nations.

demonstrated at an early age other characteristics for which he is equally well remembered. These things concern the strength of his character. He became widely known for his advocacy of the humane treatment of prisoners, at a time when warfare was waged with brutality by all parties. He demonstrated qualities of leadership and of oratorical skill while still a boy, being a natural leader that other boys followed. By the time he reached adulthood, his political ideas were well formulated, and he was very effective in articulating them.

He and Chicksika had traveled widely throughout the Midwest, visiting many tribes. The Shawnees were especially adept at diplomacy, and generations of travel and mutual contact had made them welcome visitors with tribes throughout a large region. These travels helped prepare Tecumseh for his future role.

the Ohio country, where they faced constant friction with the encroaching non-Natives. Tecumseh's older sister, Tecumpease, then assumed a large role in caring for Tecumseh until he reached adulthood.

It is not known when Tecumseh formulated the political principles of unification of a large number of Indian nations, or his belief that the land belonged to all Indians and that no one tribe had a right to sell land, but he is known to have

By 1805, his brother, Tenskwatawa (the Prophet), had begun gathering religious followers to him, whom Tecumseh converted to his political ideas. He traveled from tribe to tribe gathering followers, alarming government officials on the frontier.

In the fall of 1811, while Tecumseh was in the South unsuccessfully attempting to gain followers among the Choctaws and the Cherokees and meeting with some success among the Creeks, disaster struck back home in Ohio. U.S. General William Henry Harrison marched a group of army troops close to the Prophet's encampment. The two forces clashed, resulting in a devasting defeat for the Indi-

This colored woodcut portrays the death of Shawnee leader Tecumseh in 1813 at the Battle of the Thames in Canada.

ans. Tecumseh returned home to find his plans for a pan-Indian alliance in shambles.

Not long after, the War of 1812 broke out between Britain and the United States. Tecumseh joined the British in the war, while still attempting to pursue his idea of a political and military alliance consisting of many tribes. His vision died, however, when he was killed at the Battle of the Thames, in Canada, in 1813. His brother, the Prophet, survived him, and he was removed with other Shawnees to the West when the United States finally gained control of the Ohio Valley and forced most of the Native peoples onto reservations beyond the Mississippi River.

SEE ALSO:
Pan-Indian (Intertribal) Movements; Shawnee; Tippecanoe, Battle of.

TECUMSEH'S REBELLION AND WAR OF 1812

SEE Tecumseh.

TEEPEE

SEE Tipi.

TELEVISION

SEE Hollywood, Indians and Indian Images; Silverheels, Jay.

TENNESSEE

Tennessee became the sixteenth U.S. state on June 1, 1796. Although the exact meaning of the word *Tennessee* cannot be documented, it is believed to be an American Indian word for "great river."

In addition to providing the name for Ten-

nessee, Native Americans have also played a large part in many other ways in the story of the state. Indians have lived in the area that is now called Tennessee for a very long time. There is archaeological evidence that indicates Indians have been in the region for over five thousand years. The Mound Builder civilization was very active in the western part of Tennessee and came to an end at about the time Europeans first visited the region in the mid-1500s.

In 1541, Spanish conquistador Hernando de Soto, along with his army, became the first Europeans to enter Tennessee. Other Spanish and French settlers followed, but the first European settlement did not occur in the area until 1779, when John Sevier and James Robertson founded Watauga, near present-day Nashville.

At the time of this first permanent European settlement, there were three major tribes occupying parts of Tennessee: The Cherokees lived in the eastern part of the state, the Shawnees occupied portions of central Tennessee, and the Chickasaw people lived in western Tennessee.

Although all three tribes resisted the European invasion of their land, each tribe was forced to cede all territory in the state by the early part of the 1800s. No reservations currently exist in Tennessee.

The 1990 U.S. Census lists 10,039 Indians as state residents, which ranks Tennessee thirty-sixth among states in Native American population.

SEE ALSO:
Cherokee; Chickasaw; De Soto, Hernando; Mound Builders; Shawnee.

TENSKWATAWA

SEE Tecumseh.

TERMINATION ACT

SEE Termination Policy.

TERMINATION POLICY

In the years after World War II—following the limited easing of U.S. policies affecting the sovereignty and identity of American Indians while John Collier was commissioner of Indian Affairs under Franklin Delano Roosevelt (1933–1945)—attitudes toward Native Americans swung once again toward policies of termination. ("Termination" refers to the policies of the federal government, practiced for the most part in the 1950s, that aimed to end the protectionist policies of the U.S. government toward Indian tribes.) These policies were meant to extinguish Native Americans' land base and tribal identity.

During the 1930s and 1940s, John Collier's policies had halted a general decline in Native American populations, health, and land base, but Indian people still remained desperately poor compared to middle-class mainstream standards. Politicians assumed that obliterating "Indianness" (erasing the Indians' identity as Indians) would propel Native peoples out of poverty and out of a dependence on government that earlier Bureau of Indian Affairs (BIA) policies had created. They argued that rapid assimilation into the mainstream demanded forceful elimination of Indians' loyalty to their tribe, culture, and tribal land bases. In the late 1940s, this position reached the peak of its political expression, and a wave of terminations was enacted by the government during the 1950s. House Concurrent Resolution 108, also known as the Termination Policy, provided for the withdrawal of the U.S. government's supervision of Indian nations.

Under termination, land and resources were purchased from tribes and the proceeds were distributed to individual members. These members found themselves temporarily enriched in cash but suddenly deprived of land and community. Through various legal devices, much of the purchased land was then transferred into the private sector. This usually meant that the land found its way into non-Native hands, often through lease for a specific purpose (such as logging or mineral exploration) or outright sale.

The Indian Claims Commission, established to pay for land illegally taken from Native American peoples, was linked with the emerging termination policy by its supporters. Senator Arthur B. Watkins, architect of termination, wrote: "[The] basic purpose of Congress in setting up the Indian Claims Commission was to clear the way toward complete freedom of the Indian by assuring final settlement of all obligations—real or purported—of the Federal government to the Indian tribes."

Political momentum toward termination was accelerating as Dwight Eisenhower assumed the presidency in 1952. Eisenhower appointed Glenn L. Emmons, a supporter of Watkins's termination legislation, as commissioner of Indian affairs. Between 1953 and 1962, Congress passed legislation terminating federal recognition of tribes as independent nations and ending federal services to sixty Native nations. As a result of this legislation, some of these tribes disappeared as organized communities.

At the same time, the BIA, through its relocation program, was moving Indians to urban areas. Between 1953 and 1972, the BIA sponsored more than one hundred thousand Native people who moved from their rural homes to large cities. Isolation from home and culture would forcefully thrust Indians into mainstream culture, thus ending their identity as Indians—at least that was the purpose of the program.

Sometimes, Congress withheld claims payments for Indian lands taken illegally in the past until the Native tribe or nation in question also agreed to termination proceedings, thereby obliterating both past and present land bases. In 1963, for example, the claims commission awarded the Kalispels $3 million, an award that was held by Congress until they agreed to termination. The Klamaths, holding title to a million acres (four hundred thousand hectares) of prime timber in Oregon, were enticed into terminating after BIA agents promised them payments of $50,000 per person. Only afterward did the Klamaths painfully learn that "going private" can be expensive. They found themselves paying rent, utilities, health-care costs, and taxes they had never faced before.

The Menominees of Wisconsin shared ownership of property valued at $34 million when their termination bill was enacted in 1953. By 1961, the federal government was out of Menominee country, and each member of the former tribe had become the owner of one hundred shares of stock and a negotiable bond valued at $3,000, issued in the name of Menominee Enterprises, Inc. (MEI), a private enterprise that held the former tribe's land and businesses. Governmentally, the Menominee Nation had become Menominee County, the smallest (in terms of population) and poorest (in terms of cash income) in Wisconsin.

As a county, Menominee had to raise taxes to pay for its share of services, including welfare, health services, and utilities. The only taxable property owner in the county was MEI, which was forced to raise the funds to pay its tax bill by restructuring so that stockholders had to buy their homes and the property on which they had been built. Most of the Menominees had little savings except for their $3,000 bonds, which were then sold to MEI to make the required residential purchases. Many Menominees faced private-sector health costs, property taxes, and other expenses with no more money than they had had before termination. Unemployment rose to levels that most of the United States had known only during the 1930s (the era of the Great Depression). By 1965, health indicators in Menominee County sounded like a reprint of the Meriam Report (a report released in 1928 that gave dramatic evidence of the need to improve health and social services to Native people) of almost four decades earlier. Tuberculosis afflicted nearly 35 percent of the population, and infant mortality was three times the national average. Termination, like allotment, had been an abject failure at anything other than separating Indians from their land, and then selling of the land.

Many opponents of termination were Native traditionalists, who insisted that Native cultures and land bases should be maintained. An Indian agent at Colville in northeastern Washington reported how Native people under his "wardship" looked at termination proposals: "They seem to feel that the program is a government means to move the Indians from the reservation in order to allow white operators to exploit the reservation and eventually force all the Indians from the reservation areas."

At the same time that the termination legislation was enacted, the National Congress of American Indians (NCAI) began to organize. The group formed in 1944 at an initial convention in Denver. The NCAI worked to assist the claims commission but strongly opposed termination. The group fought termination by bringing several hundred Native Americans to Capitol Hill to argue against this policy but failed to prevent enactment of the new law. In 1954, after termination had become law, NCAI bitterly denounced it at a convention in Omaha. In 1958, NCAI President Joseph Garry characterized termination as the worst federal policy since the beginning of the twentieth century.

During the 1950s' Red Scare (a witch-hunt for communists in the government, arts, and other sectors of society) led by Senator Joseph McCarthy, Native tribalism was often attacked by conservatives as communistic. Those who made this argument claimed that the nature of tribalism, with its emphasis on community and on a national identity in addition to that of the United States of America, posed a threat to U.S. democracy. The efforts of conservatives to terminate Native cultural identity received unexpected support from some liberals who might normally be expected to support the rights of Native peoples. These liberals, examining the Supreme Court's ruling in *Brown v. Board of Education* (the 1954 landmark legislation that paved the way for the civil rights movement by prohibiting "separate but equal" education for the races), began to argue that reservations constituted a form of segregation produced by law.

For years following this era, the policy of termination would produce the same result as allotment—the loss of lands for Native Americans. And with that loss of land came a loss of tribal identity and security. By the late 1960s and early 1970s, it had become clear that the policy of termination had been, for the most part, a failure, bringing added poverty and instability into the lives of American Indians. Today, many Indian groups have regained their status as federally recognized tribes, and many more are in the process of petitioning the government to have their status restored.

— B. E. Johansen

SEE ALSO:

Acculturation; Bureau of Indian Affairs; Collier, John; Federal Recognition; General Allotment Act; House Concurrent Resolution 108; Indian Claims Commission Act; Menominee; Meriam, Lewis; Relocation Program; Wardship.

SUGGESTED READINGS:

Davis, Mary B., ed. *Native America in the Twentieth Century.* New York: Garland Publishing, 1994.

Gates, Paul, ed. *The Rape of Indian Lands.* New York: Arno Press, 1979.

Josephy, Alvin M., Jr. *Now That the Buffalo's Gone: A Study of Today's American Indians.* New York: Knopf, 1982.

Levitan, Sar A. *Big Brother's Indian Programs—with Reservations.* New York: McGraw-Hill, 1971.

McNickle, D'Arcy. *They Came Here First: The Epic of the American Indians.* New York: Harper Perennial Library, 1975.

Olson, James S., and Raymond Wilson. *Native Americans in the Twentieth Century.* Urbana: University of Illinois Press, 1984.

Parman, Donald L. *Indians and the American West in the Twentieth Century.* Bloomington: Indiana University Press, 1994.

TESTING, NUCLEAR

The U.S. government began developing nuclear weapons during World War II with its top-secret Manhattan Project. By August of 1945, the United States was able to drop the world's first atomic bombs on the Japanese cities of Hiroshima and Nagasaki, causing Japan's almost immediate surrender.

During the Cold War and nuclear arms race of the 1950s, the U.S. government's Atomic Energy Commission (AEC) stepped up the program. From 1951 to 1959, the United States dropped 126 atomic bombs within its own borders on a 1,350-square-mile (3,510-square-kilometer) area officially designated as the Nevada test site. While the AEC had 37 active secret installations throughout the country, their central laboratory was located in Los Alamos, New Mexico, near the Nevada testing site. Over 100,000 people, including thousands of the government's top nuclear scientists and engineers, worked at this site both to oversee the blasts and to conduct tests to measure the aftereffects of the subsequent atomic radiation fallout.

The Nevada test site was chosen for two reasons: its sparse population density and the ease with which the government could take it over. In secret documents from the early 1950s, it was revealed that the AEC officially referred to the people living there (mostly Native Americans and Mormons) as "a low-use segment of the population." These people also came to be known as the "Downwinders" because they were in the direct path of the atomic fallout clouds that mushroomed into the atmosphere after the blasts.

It soon became obvious that radiation fallout affected far more people than those living within the 1,350-square-mile (3,510-square-kilometer) test site. Typically, a fallout cloud drifted through Death Valley to much of Southern California, as well as in other directions, covering most if not all of the states of Nevada, Utah, and Arizona.

As for the test site itself, the land was legally owned by the Western Shoshone. Yet, without any consultation or negotiation with Shoshone leaders for rights or permission, President Harry Truman simply issued a presidential proclamation in 1951 that declared the territory the official testing site for nuclear bombs. The inhabitants of the two major reservations in the immediate testing area suffered (and will continue to suffer) some of the severest affects from tests of the 1950s. These are the Shoshones living on the Stillwater Reservation in northern Nevada and the Paiutes on the Shivwits Reservation just west of St. George, Utah.

The radiation fallout burned and killed hundreds of thousands of farm animals, poisoned the fish in the surrounding lakes and rivers, and contaminated soil and waterways as far away as Maine and Virginia. Thousands of soldiers and civilians around the Nevada test site during the 1950s suffered disfiguring burns and blindness. But some of the most horrific aftereffects did not start to appear until a few years after the tests had started. Mothers who had been exposed to radiation later gave birth to babies with physical deformities and other anomalies. The death rates from cancer, diabetes, and thyroid disease skyrocketed, particularly among those living on the nearby reservations. So did the incidence of blindness, nervous system disorders, blood vessel diseases, and osteoporosis, a disease in which the bones become extremely porous, leading to increases in fractures and slow healing. (On the Shivwits Reservation, 60 percent of the population now have type one diabetes.)

AEC scientists developed and tested the first hydrogen bomb in November of 1952, beating the Soviet Union by almost a year. The AEC monitored the aftereffects of their blasts all over the Southwest. Their mission had been to create a highly destructive, demoralizing weapon, and they soon discovered how well they had succeeded. A well-aimed nuclear bomb could do much more than instantly kill several million people. In spite of their extensive knowledge of its toxic effects, however, the AEC continued to issue statements to the American public stating that radiation was not a problem. And they did not limit their testing to bomb aftereffects.

Some of the AEC's most controversial testing took place at their Hanford facility in Oregon in the early 1950s in which they injected human subjects with tritium and radioiron, then analyzed samples of their bone, liver, and lung tissues. Scientists at Hanford were the first to successfully use plutonium injections to produce lung tumors and the first to study the effects of strontium-90 on metabolism and fetal growth. The subjects of these experiments were not just animals but included site employees, medical patients, and people with mental disorders.

Not all of the U.S. government's secret testing took place within the United States. A physiological study was conducted in the Peruvian Andes in late 1952 in which healthy Peruvian Indians were injected with various levels of radiotoxic chemicals to study the effects of radiation on enemy personnel at high altitudes. This study was supported by the U.S. Atomic Energy Commission, the United States Navy, and the United States Air Force.

Neither the AEC's bomb blasts nor their covert biological testing went unchallenged by victims and concerned community groups, but the government went to such great lengths to deny the secret activities that the truth did not begin to attract national public attention until the 1980s. By the 1970s, the manufacture and testing of nuclear weapons had become a $4-billion-a-year industry, with seventeen nuclear plants staffed by over 120,000 employees. AEC officials and nuclear industry leaders successfully demanded that potentially incriminating documents had to remain top secret in the interests of national security.

Finally, in 1978, President Jimmy Carter ordered the AEC's records to be made public and ordered a congressional investigation. The public began to hear disturbing truths, not just about the long-covered-up aftereffects of radiation fallout, but about the nuclear industry's dangerously deteriorating equipment, its alarming safety record, and the disastrous effects of chemical and radioactive pollution on the environment. Also, by the late 1980s, the need for nuclear arms seemed less pressing to the U.S. public as communism was collapsing in Eastern Europe and the Cold War was coming to an end.

Starting with the area around the Nevada test site, communities in every state with a nuclear facility began demanding an end to the manufacture and testing of radioactive materials. The House Judiciary Committee held hearings on everything from the massive radiation deaths of Utah sheep in the 1950s to the alarming number of cancer-related deaths since then (especially in children) in people living on or near the Nevada test site.

In 1988, Congress directed the Department of Veterans Affairs to provide disability benefits to army veterans with cancer who had participated in atmospheric testing in Nevada. And in October of 1990, President Bush signed the Radiation Exposure Act to officially apologize for the government's behavior in the Southwest and to establish a trust fund for the injured. In states such as Washington, Oregon, and Idaho, the U.S. Centers for Disease Control and Prevention and the National Center for Environmental Health are working in collaboration with Indian nations to distribute information to people whose families lived on or near the Nevada testing site after 1950. For most of the victims, however, these efforts have been too little and too late.

Also in 1990, the United States stopped manufacturing nuclear bombs and agreed to only test them underground. Most of the plants have already been closed; only two will remain in operation to oversee the dismantling of the thousands of nuclear warheads built since 1950. On July 31, 1991, U.S. President George Bush and Soviet Union President Mikhail Gorbachev signed the first Strategic Arms Reduction Treaty (START I), an agreement to reduce land-based intercontinental ballistic missiles. A second START treaty (START II) was signed by Bush and Russian President Boris Yeltsin on January 3, 1993.

— P. Press

SEE ALSO:

Paiute; Shoshone; Uranium Mining (Navajo).

SUGGESTED READINGS:

Ball, Howard. *Justice Downwind—America's Atomic Testing Program in the 1950s.* New York: Oxford University Press, 1986.

Fradkin, Philip L. *Fallout: An American Nuclear Tragedy.* Tucson: University of Arizona Press, 1989.

Saffer, Thomas H., and Orvilee E. Kelly. *Countdown Zero.* New York: G. P. Putnam's Sons, 1982.

TEWA PUEBLOS

The Pueblo people of New Mexico are members of three distinct language families— Keresan, Zunian, and Tanoan; the Tanoan language is divided into three dialects—Tiwa, Towa, and Tewa. Six pueblos speak the Tewa dialect— Nambé, Pojoaque, Santa Clara, San Ildefonso, San Juan, and Tesuque. All are northern pueblos located north of Santa Fe.

Nambé Pueblo is located in an area of scenic land formations. The pueblo has 19,124 acres (7,745 hectares) of land. Population statistics for the pueblo have varied over the past two decades. The 1980 census reported a population of 438, and the 1989 Bureau of Indian Affairs (BIA) Labor Force Report listed the population at 435. However, the 1990 census reported a population of 1,369. Arts and crafts are available at the pueblo, but permits must be purchased if photographs are to be taken.

Pojoaque Pueblo has 11,601 acres (4,698 hectares) of land. The 1980 census reported a population of 124, and the 1989 BIA Labor Force Report listed the population at 102. However, the 1990 census reported the population at 2,463. A late nineteenth-century smallpox epidemic almost

A photograph by Edward S. Curtis of a nineteenth-century Tewa girl.

Two youngsters at a San Ildefonso Pueblo feast day.

destroyed Pojoaque. The present settlement dates from the 1930s, but ruins of the original pueblo are nearby. Also nearby are the ruins of several pueblos abandoned after the Pueblo Revolt of 1680. Traditional dances were revived in 1973 after having been abandoned for about a century. Revenues from a commercial strip along the highway makes Pojoaque one of the more affluent pueblos.

Santa Clara Pueblo has 45,827 acres (18,560 hectares) of land. The 1980 census reported a population of 1,374, and the 1989 BIA Labor Force Report listed the population at 1,582. However, the 1990 census reported the population at 9,640. Traditional crafts may be purchased at the pueblo, and tours are available for the ancient 740-room Puye Cliff Dwellings. Cameras are allowed by permit.

San Ildefonso Pueblo has 26,198 acres (10,610 hectares) of land. The 1980 census reported a population of 520, and the 1989 BIA Labor Force Report listed the population at 632. The 1990 census reported the population at 1,457. San Ildefonso is famous for its pottery and is host to the annual Eight Northern Indian Pueblos Artist and Craftsman Show. There is a visitor center and a museum. Cameras are not allowed at some dances.

San Juan Pueblo has 12,236 acres (4,956 hectares) of land. The 1980 census reported the population at 1,806, and the 1989 BIA Labor Force Report listed it at 1,935. The 1990 census reported the population at 4,783. San Juan Pueblo was the site of the first Spanish capital of New Mexico. Traditional crafts are available, but photography and sketching are allowed only by permit.

Tesuque Pueblo has 16,813 acres (6,809 hectares) of land. The 1980 census reported a population of 312, and the 1989 BIA Labor Force Report listed it at 328; the 1990 census reported the population at 696. The Pueblo Revolt of 1680 started here. Traditional crafts are available for purchase at the pueblo, which is listed on the National Register of Historic Places. Cameras are allowed by permit.

TEXAS

After centuries of being under Spanish rule as a part of New Spain, Texas became part of Mexico following Mexican independence, which was achieved in 1821. Following a war between U.S. settlers and the Mexican government, Texas achieved independence as the Republic of Texas in 1836. It became the twenty-eighth U.S. state on December 29, 1845.

There is some debate about where the state's name comes from. It derives from either the Spanish term *tejas*, which means "friends," or the Commanche Indian word *techas*, which means "allies." In addition to perhaps providing Texas with its name, Indians have also been involved with this area in many other ways. Archaeological evidence points out that Texas was an important meeting place for early Native cultures, and the Mesoamerican cultures of Mexico and Central America and Mound Builder Culture blended in Texas.

The first Europeans to enter the region were Alonso Alvarez de Piñeda and his party in 1519. Alvar Núñez Cabeza de Vaca and Francisco Coro-

The Old Ysleta (also spelled Isleta) Mission at Tigua Pueblo, El Paso, exemplifies the mix of Spanish colonial and Pueblo influences in Texas.

The Virgin of Guadalupe shrine at the Old Ysleta Mission, Tigua Pueblo, El Paso, Texas. Ysleta was the first permanent European settlement in Texas.

nado followed soon after, and throughout the 1600s, many Spanish explorers visited Texas. In 1682, the first permanent European settlement was founded at Ysleta (also spelled Isleta). At the time of this settlement, three major tribes called Texas their home: the Apaches, the Caddos, and the Comanches.

During the 1700s and early 1800s, other Native peoples moved into parts of Texas after being pushed west. These tribes included the Alabamas, the Lenapes (Delawares), the Shawnees, and the Cherokees. Some of these tribes signed treaties with the government of Mexico, which awarded them territory in Texas.

The Apaches, the Comanches, the Kiowas, the Kiowa Apaches, and the Southern Cheyennes violently opposed the European settlement of their lands. In 1874, Indian resistance in Texas suffered major setbacks at the Battle of Adobe Wells and the capture of the Indian stronghold in Palo Duro Canyon by General R. S. Mackenzie and his forces. Most of the Texas Indians were removed to reservations in Indian Territory (present-day Oklahoma).

Currently, three small reservations exist in Texas. These reservations are Isleta Del Sur Pueblo, the Alabama-Coushatta Reservation, and the Kickapoo Reservation.

The 1990 U.S. Census lists 65,877 Indians as state residents, which ranks Texas tenth among states in Native American population.

SEE ALSO:
Apache; Cabeza de Vaca, Alvar Núñez; Caddo; Cherokee; Cheyenne; Comanche; Coronado Expedition; Kickapoo; Kiowa; Kiowa-Apache; Lenape; Mexican-American War; Mexico, Indigenous People of; Mound Builders; Shawnee; Texas Indians; Texas Rangers.

TEXAS INDIANS

Edward S. Curtis, in volume 19 of *The North American Indian*, succinctly states the nineteenth-century Texas attitude regarding Indians: "Texas was generous in respect to its aboriginal inhabitants, being ever willing to give its Indians to any one who might want them. In fact, the Texas mandate, though not recorded in the statutes was, 'Go elsewhere or be exterminated.'" Texas expelled its aboriginal inhabitants well before the end of the 1800s, with the exception of the Natives of the ninety-seven-acre (thirty-nine-hectare) Isleta del Sur Pueblo near El Paso, the Alabama-Coushatta, and a small group of Kickapoo. It made no difference whether the Native Texas peoples were hos-

A member of the Tigua, a Texas tribe, at a ceremonial event in full regalia.

tile or friendly, nomadic or sedentary, whether they lived on the high Plains, the central Plains, the eastern woodlands, or along the Gulf shore. No difference whether they attempted to reside peacefully on land specifically set aside for them or whether they were allies of Texas, even if they had supplied fighting men to help champion the Texas cause against other Indians. They were not wanted; they were not tolerated; they were driven out of Texas or they were exterminated.

At least one prominent official who attempted to intervene on behalf of the Indians, Texas Superintendent of Indian Affairs Robert S. Neighbors, was murdered. He had committed the offense of hurriedly ushering his charges out of state in 1859 to save them from being exterminated by angry mobs who did not care to attempt any distinction between peaceful and hostile Indians. These Indians numbered about fifteen hundred, with one thousand of them being mostly Caddos, Anadarkos, Ionis, Wacos, and Tonkawas from the Brazos Reservation, and about five hundred of them being Penateka Comanches from a smaller reservation nearby. They were forced to abandon nearly all their possessions and livestock on more than seventy thousand acres (twenty-eight thousand hectares), where they had pursued an agricultural and range cattle economy, and where they had, in fact, been allies of Texas in armed engagements against other Indians. Neighbors made the mistake of returning to Texas, where he met with vigilante justice: a shotgun blast in the back.

The Cherokees, Delawares, Kickapoos, Seminoles, Shawnees, and other Native peoples from east of the Mississippi who had migrated to the headwaters of the Sabine, where they established agricultural communities, made the mistake of residing on rich land coveted by the East Texans. In 1838, they were summarily ordered to leave. When they refused, they were driven from Texas in two bloody engagements, finding themselves relentlessly pursued until they had crossed the Red River into the Choctaw and Chickasaw Nations in Indian Territory (present-day Oklahoma).

The Karankawas of the Gulf Coast, hemmed in on all sides, unable to flee and unwilling to attempt much of an accommodation with the Texans, were exterminated. One can seek out the fate of any particular Native people in Texas, but, with the exception of the Alabama-Coushatta, Isleta del Sur Pueblo and Kickapoo, the story has the same ending; they were exterminated or they were driven out.

Not until the twentieth century did Indians begin returning to Texas, where they remain practically invisible, clustered in the state's urban centers. There they struggle with the problems of urban Indians everywhere. Stripped of their land base, isolated from their scattered people, they are aliens in their native land. Being invisible, they are ignored. When they are not invisible, they are not appreciated.

Not all Texans were Indian haters bent on driving all Indians out of Texas. The Indians had a friend in Sam Houston. During his terms of office as president of the Republic of Texas and as governor of Texas when it became a U.S. state, Houston attempted to accommodate the needs of Indians in Texas governmental policy. Other prominent Texans, such as frontier physician and naturalist Dr. Gideon Lincecum, were deeply interested in Indian culture. Before moving to Texas shortly after it became a state, Lincecum had been a student of Choctaw language and culture in Mississippi. In his later years, he contributed a valuable biography of Choctaw Chief Pushmataha, as well as other observations about Choctaw culture in transition that are available nowhere else. (Lincecum's contributions were published early in the twentieth century in the *Publications of the Mississippi Historical Society*.) One of the most sympathetic and knowledgeable students of Choctaw culture, H. B. Cushman, grew up among the Choctaws of Mississippi early in the nineteenth century as the son of American Board missionaries to the Choctaws and spent his mature years as a resident of Texas. (Cushman's *History of the Choctaw, Chickasaw, and Natchez Indians*, 1899, is a cherished document for students of Choctaw history.)

But people such as these were a distinct minority in Texas. Even Sam Houston, while president of the Republic of Texas, was unable to persuade the Texas Senate to ratify the treaty he had negotiated on February 25, 1836, with the Sabine River communities of Eastern Indians. In 1838, Houston's successor, Mirabeau Lamar, moved quickly to drive those communities out of Texas.

The experience of Native peoples in Texas is illustrative of how non-Native attitudes toward

Indians had hardened by the time Texas achieved independence from Mexico and by the time it was granted statehood. By that time, many Indian nations from east of the Mississippi had been forcibly evicted from their ancestral homelands and removed to Indian Territory. Indian allies were no longer needed against rival colonial powers. The doctrine of Manifest Destiny (which held that it was the "destiny" of the United States to fulfill its nature by expanding across the continent as far as the Pacific) had taken deep root in the U.S. national character, and the rights of indigenous peoples were no part of that doctrine, either in theory or in practice.

— D. L. Birchfield

SEE ALSO:

Manifest Destiny; Mexican-American War; Mexico; Pueblo; Pushmataha; Texas; Texas Rangers.

SUGGESTED READINGS:

Curtis, Edward S. *The North American Indian*, vol. 19. New York: Johnson Reprint Corporation, 1978; c. 1907–1908.

Newcomb, W. W., Jr. *The Indians of Texas: From Prehistoric to Modern Times*. Austin: University of Texas Press, 1961.

Richardson, Rupert Norval. *Texas: The Lone Star State*. 4th ed. Englwood Cliffs, NJ: Prentice-Hall, 1981.

TEXAS RANGERS

When Hardin R. Runnels became governor of the state of Texas on December 21, 1857, official Texas policy became one of genocidal attack upon Indians, even if the Indians were to be found living outside the boundaries of Texas. The Texas legislature approved the creation of a new company of one hundred Texas Rangers specifically designated for offensive operations.

United States Army policy in Texas had been one of maintaining a defensive line of fortifications stretching across West Texas. This policy changed quickly after the Texas Rangers demonstrated that Plains Indian villages filled with women and children were in no way defensible military fortifications.

Governor Runnels appointed Ranger Captain John S. "Rip" Ford as senior captain in charge of all Texas forces and commissioned him to pursue the Indians to wherever he might find them, brooking no interference from the United States or anyone else. These forces consisted of 102 Texas Rangers, most of them armed with two Colt pistols and a muzzle-loading rifle, giving them an estimated firepower of fifteen hundred rounds without reloading, and an equal or slightly greater number of Indian auxiliaries from the Brazos Reservation under the command of Captain Shapley P. Ross. With these men, Ford crossed the Red River into present-day Oklahoma and, in the early morning hours of May 12, 1858, attacked without warning and destroyed a Comanche village on the north bank of the Canadian River near the Antelope Hills, killing more than seventy people.

Regarding this attack, Rupert Norval Richardson writes in *The Comanche Barrier to South Plains Settlement*, "The village which was destroyed was that of a band of Kotsoteka or Buffalo-eater Comanches. The fact that there were no 'American' horses among the three hundred or more head which Ford and Ross took from the village indicates that this Comanche band had not recently committed depredations on the Texas settlements. Ford does not state the number of women and children among the seventy-six Indians slain, for that was a matter of no great concern to the Texas people. . . . A singular characteristic of the Ford-Ross campaign is that it was carried out by Texas forces, acting on state authority only, yet operating and fighting a battle outside of the state. In this regard, the officers take no notice of the fact that the battle with the Indians was not fought on Texas soil, and the boundary line evidently was a matter of little concern to them. The Indians had been defeated; the place of the engagement and the means used were items of little consequence. As one enthusiastic citizen wrote the president: 'The rangers, with the assistance of the friendly Indians, killed seventy wild Indians. When did the soldiers ever do as much?' "

Contemplating this genocide, Walter Prescott Webb writes in *The Texas Rangers*, "In Ford's eyes the campaign was of much importance. It had demonstrated that the Indians could be followed, found, and defeated in their own country; it proved

A group of Texas Rangers on horseback (note the early automobile in the background), photographed in the early 1900s.

that the buffalo ranges beyond Red River could be penetrated and held by white men."

Captain Ford's attack showed the United States Army how vulnerable the Plains Indians were in their villages. It was a lesson the army was not long in taking to heart. Major General David E. Twiggs, of the U.S. Army's Department of Texas, was inspired by the example set before him, as Robert Utley reports in *Frontiersmen in Blue*. " 'For the last ten years we have been on the defensive,' he wrote to General [Winfield] Scott on July 6. Now it was time to abandon this policy, invade the Indian homeland, and 'follow them up winter and summer, thus giving the Indians something to do at home in taking care of their families, and they might possibly let Texas alone.' "

On October 1, 1858, acting on orders from General Twiggs, Major Earl Van Dorn, leading a force of United States Cavalry out of Texas into present-day Oklahoma, attacked and destroyed a

joint encampment of Wichitas and Comanches near the present town of Rush Springs. Unknown to General Twiggs and Major Van Dorn, these Indians had just concluded an agreement of peace and friendship with officers from Fort Arbuckle of the U.S. Army's Department of the West. General Twiggs and Mayor Van Dorn were embarrassed by this difficulty in following the Texas Rangers' example of shooting first and asking questions later. Their response was to urge that the army put a stop to such treaty making. Early the next year, Major Van Dorn carried out another attack from Texas, this time on Comanches in present-day southern Kansas.

The beginning of the end for the Plains Indians, at least on the Southern Plains, can be traced to this genocidal military tactic of the Texas Rangers, first demonstrated in the spring of 1858. Many other factors would be important in the destruction of the Plains Indians' way of life, among them the eventual slaughter of the buffalo herds upon which their culture depended. But the vulnerability of their women and children in their villages played a significant role in breaking their will to resist, and the Texas Rangers played the leading role in inaugurating that genocidal tactic.

— D. L. Birchfield

SEE ALSO:

Oklahoma; Texas Indians.

SUGGESTED READINGS:

Hughes, W. J. *Rebellious Ranger: Rip Ford and the Old Southwest.* Norman: University of Oklahoma Press, 1979.

Maltby, William Jeff. *Captain Jeff: Or Frontier Life in Texas with the Texas Rangers* (1906). Waco, TX: Texian Press, 1967.

Richardson, Rupert Norval. *The Comanche Barrier to South Plains Settlement: A Century and a Half of Savage Resistance to the Advancing White Frontier.* Glendale, CA: Arthur H. Clark Company, 1933.

Samora, Julian, Joe Bernal, and Albert Pena. *Gunpowder Justice: A Reassessment of the Texas Rangers.* Notre Dame, IN: University of Notre Dame Press, 1979.

Utley, Robert M. *Frontiersmen in Blue: The United States Army and the Indian, 1848–1865.* New York: Macmillan, 1967.

THANKSGIVING

Ceremonies of thanksgiving for the bounty of nature are a common element in many Native American cultures, including the people who introduced the custom to the New England colonists, or Pilgrims, in 1621. A fall thanksgiving holiday, usually accompanied by feasting on such traditional Native American foods as turkey, corn, yams, squashes, and cranberry sauce, has been widely practiced since about 1800 by most non-Native people in the United States and Canada. Thanksgiving was declared a national holiday by President Abraham Lincoln in 1863 in the midst of the Civil War. Canada declared an official Thanksgiving holiday in 1879; this day is celebrated six weeks before its counterpart in the United States.

Contrary to popular belief, the Pilgrims were not the first Europeans to eat turkey. Turkeys were first domesticated by the Aztecs and imported to Spain during the conquest more than a century before English colonists arrived in New England. Aztec turkeys had been imported to England by the time the Pilgrims sailed, and the immigrants had some of the birds on board.

This painting by J. L. G. Ferris of the first Thanksgiving depicts English settlers and local Indians in an atmosphere of goodwill in 1621 New England, well before it became an official holiday in the United States, in 1863, and in Canada, in 1879.

This view of a Native American Alternative Thanksgiving Day parade combines many images of a culturally diverse North America: An African-American girl marches alongside a U.S. flag with an Indian figure superimposed over the Stars and Stripes; behind the flag is a banner calling for a halt to a hydroelectric project threatening Native lands in Quebec, Canada.

A spirit of thanksgiving to the natural world is common in many Native cultures, as reflected in the following prayer offered by Tom Porter, a Mohawk Nation Council subchief : "[Before] our great-great grandfathers were first born and given the breath of life, our Creator at that time said the earth will be your mother. And the Creator said to the deer, and the animals and the birds, the earth will be your mother, too. And I have instructed the earth to give food and nourishment and medicine and quenching of thirst to all life. . . . We, the people, humbly thank you today, mother earth."

He continued, "You must have a reverence and great respect for your mother the earth. . . . . You must each day say 'thank you' [for] every gift that contributes to your life. If you follow this pattern, it will [be] like a circle with no end. Your life will be as everlasting as your children will carry on your flesh, your blood, and your heartbeat."

A tribute to the Creator and a reverence for the natural world is also reflected in many Native greetings that span the North American conti-nent. More than 2,500 miles (4,025 kilometers) from the homeland of the Mohawks, the Lummis of the Pacific Northwest Coast might begin a public meeting this way: "To the Creator, Great Spirit, Holy Father: may the words that we share here today give the people and [generations] to come the understanding of the sacredness of all life and creation."

SEE ALSO:

Aztec; Ecology, Native American Conception of; First Salmon Ceremony; Green Corn Ceremony

THORPE, GRACE (1921–)

Grace Thorpe is a highly regarded Indian rights activist and the daughter of world-famous athlete Jim Thorpe. She was born in 1921 in Yale, Oklahoma. A Sac (Sauk) and Fox, Thorpe is a descendant of Chief Black Hawk.

Throughout most of her life, Thorpe has been involved in a wide range of activities that have put her in the midst of many significant events. During World War II, she was stationed in New Guinea as a member of the Women's Army Corps. She joined General Douglas MacArthur's staff at the command headquarters in Japan.

By the mid-1960s, Thorpe had become active in many groups involved with Native issues, including land acquisition, government, public relations, and community organizations. In 1966, she helped obtain property in California for Deganawidah-Quetzalcoatl (or D-Q) University, designed to meet the specific needs of Indian and Latino students. (The university derived its name from Deganawidah and Quetzalcoatl, two figures in Iroquois and Aztec tradition, respectively, who are emblems of the incredible diversity of Native cultures in the Americas.)

Also in the 1960s, Thorpe spent a year with the National Council of American Indians and participated in the activist occupations of Alcatraz Island in California and the Fort Lawton Museum in Washington State. She also helped organize the National Indian Women's Action Corps and served as a legislative assistant to the United States Senate Subcommittee on Indian Affairs. She spent two years with the American Indian Policy Review Board sponsored by the U.S. House of Representatives.

Thorpe received her paralegal certification from

Famed Sac and Fox athlete Jim Thorpe and his daughter, Grace, at the Haskell Institute in Lawrence, Kansas, in 1931. Each had been a student at Haskell.

Antioch School of Law in 1974, before receiving her bachelor's degree from the University of Tennessee, Knoxville, in 1980. Also in 1980, she returned to Oklahoma, where she serves as a part-time district court judge for the Five Tribes in Stroud. She is also vice president of the Jim Thorpe Foundation and managed to secure the return of her father's Olympic medals to the Thorpe family. Inspired by her father's life and her efforts to restore dignity to his memory, she wrote the "Jim Thorpe Family History: 1750–1904," which was published in *Chronicles of Oklahoma*.

Jim Thorpe had won gold medals in the pentathlon and decathlon as a member of the 1912 U.S. Olympic team. It was later learned that Thorpe had briefly played semiprofessional baseball to earn money during his college years, and in 1913, the Amateur Athletic Union stripped him of his amateur status and took his medals back. Before he died in 1953, he was elected to the Pro Football Hall of Fame in Canton, Ohio, but it was not until 1983, thirty years after his death, that Grace Thorpe would succeed in restoring his medals to her family.

Grace Thorpe continues to be very active in the Indian rights movement. She is also an environmental activist and was instrumental in creating a nuclear free zone in the Sac and Fox tribal jurisdiction in Oklahoma.

SEE ALSO:

Alcatraz Island, Occupation of; Black Hawk; D-Q University; Sac and Fox; Thorpe, Jim.

THORPE, JIM

Sac and Fox athlete Jim Thorpe is regarded as one of the greatest athletes of all time. He dominated the 1912 Summer Olympics in Stockholm, Sweden, after which the *New York Times* proclaimed him to be the world's greatest all-around athlete. He achieved many other athletic distinctions during a long career that included both professional football and baseball. In a 1950 Associated Press poll, Thorpe was voted both the greatest male athlete and the greatest American football player of the first half of the twentieth century.

He was born on May 22, 1887, on the Sac and Fox Nation near present-day Prague, Oklahoma. Jim Thorpe had a twin brother, named Charlie, who died of pneumonia at the age of nine. At the age of six, the twins had begun attending the Sac and Fox Mission School. Jim had other siblings, both older and younger, but the death of his twin brother affected him deeply. It was a loss he would feel for the rest of his life.

After mission school, Jim Thorpe attended Haskell Institute, in Lawrence, Kansas, for three years, until he ran away from the school and returned home on his own in 1901. While at Haskell, he first learned the game of football, but he was too young to participate on the varsity team.

His father, however, insisted that he complete his education, and so in 1904 he was sent to Pennsylvania to the Carlisle Industrial Indian School. In his last two years at Carlisle, he was selected to the All-America football team. In the 1912 season, he played against a future president of the United States in the Army game, cadet Dwight Eisenhower, who in later years would say that Jim Thorpe was the greatest athlete he had ever known. In that same season, Thorpe set a college record by scoring 198 points.

In the 1912 Summer Olympics, he won gold medals in both the pentathlon (consisting of five track and field events) and the decathlon (consisting of ten track and field events). His record performance in the decathlon was not broken for thirty-six years. Within six months of the Olympics, however, Thorpe was stripped of his medals, because he had played semiprofessional baseball in 1909 and 1910. In 1982, nearly thirty years after his death, Thorpe's medals were restored to his family by the International Olympic Committee, which ruled that the meager pay he had received while playing baseball (fifteen dollars per week) should not have changed his standing as an amateur athlete.

After the Olympics, Thorpe played professional baseball for the New York Giants and the Boston Braves until 1919, reaching the World Series with the Giants in 1917, which they lost in six games. At the same time, beginning in 1915, he played professional football. He played for many different teams, achieving great distinction in the sport, until his retirement in 1929. In 1919, he served as the first president of the American Professional Football Association, which later changed its name to the National Football League (NFL).

Thorpe remained active as a lecturer and sports promoter for the rest of his life. In 1949, a movie was made about his life titled *Jim Thorpe—All American*, starring Burt Lancaster as Jim Thorpe. Thorpe died of a heart attack on March 28, 1953, in California, at the age of sixty-four.

SEE ALSO:

Baseball; Carlisle Indian School; Haskell Indian Nations University; Sac and Fox; Thorpe, Grace.

Jim Thorpe with the New York Giants, sometime before 1920. At the time this photo was taken, Thorpe was also playing pro football.

THUNDER CLOUD, RED
(c. 1920–1996)

Red Thunder Cloud (Catawba), also known as Carlos Westez, was a singer, storyteller, and dancer who earned a living by packaging and selling his own line of teas and herbs that he gathered in the wooded area around his home in Worcester, Massachusetts. Thunder Cloud will probably be best remembered as a living library of American Indian history and tradition and, especially, as the last known living speaker of the Catawba language.

Catawba belongs to the Siouan language family. According to anthropology and linguistics scholars, Catawba was, like many Native tongues, a victim of the prejudice that often beset Native speakers who were looked down upon by non-Indians. This reluctance to use Catawba for fear of being set apart may also have been encouraged by Mormon missionaries who came into the Catawba community in South Carolina with the intent of converting the Catawbas.

In the 1940s, the Massachusetts Institute of Technology produced a recording of Thunder Cloud speaking all he knew of the Catawba language. Around the same time, he also recorded several ancient Catawba songs for the Smithsonian Institution in Washington, D.C., and he made several other records of Catawba songs and legends in 1990.

According to his friends, Red Thunder Cloud learned the Catawba language as a boy from his grandfather, Strong Eagle, and other tribal elders. As the years went on, the only Catawba speakers left were Thunder Cloud and a woman who is believed to have died in the 1940s. Today, Catawba population estimates range from several hundred to more than one thousand, but none of the known tribal members speaks the ancient Catawba language.

In a story printed in the *New York Times* on January 14, 1996, about a week after his death, several of Red Thunder Cloud's companions told stories about their old friend. Foxx Ayers of Columbia, South Carolina, a Catawba himself, related an amusing anecdote about one of his brief experiences with the Catawba language. One day many years ago, attempting to deliver an armful of pottery made by Ayers's wife, who is also a Catawba, he found his entrance to Thunder Cloud's home blocked by Thunder Cloud's dog. Knowing that the dog responded only to commands spoken in Catawba, Ayers attempted a phrase that he had heard Thunder Cloud use: "Swie hay, tany," which translates as "Move, dog." The dog moved.

SEE ALSO:
Siouan Languages.

TIPI

A tipi is a cone-shaped tent that was home and shelter to the tribes of the Great Plains, such as the Blackfeet, Cheyenne, Crow, and Lakota. Because the Plains Indians were a migratory people who followed the path of the buffalo, the tipi was ideal for their nomadic way of life.

The word *tipi* means "used to dwell in." The word derives from two Dakota words, *ti*, meaning "to dwell," and *pi*, which means, "used for."

The structure of the tipi may appear quite simple, but in fact, it is a cleverly engineered and serviceable home. The tipi is well lighted and well ventilated, cool in the summer and cozy in the winter. It is designed to be sturdy in high winds, and it remains dry in heavy rains. Moreover, the tipi is quickly and easily set up and taken down.

The tipi is constructed of a frame of wooden poles arranged in a cone shape. Traditionally, the framework was enclosed by a cover of buffalo hides, but modern tipis are covered with canvas. The cone shape is very practical as it withstands strong winds; because it has no pockets or folds to catch water, it easily sheds rain.

An open fire is placed in the center of the tipi and provides warmth and light, as well as a stove for indoor cooking. The smoke from the fire is vented from an opening at the top of the tipi. Two flaps extend from the cover at the smoke hole and are attached to two poles on the outside of the lodge. By moving the poles to adjust the flaps, wind and rain are kept out, and the flaps can be crossed to close the smoke hole.

The number of poles depend upon the size of the tipi. On average, a tipi consists of fifteen poles over twenty feet (six meters) long for the frame and two more for the smoke flaps. Every tipi needs a foundation that provides underlying support for the

These contemporary tipis are painted with designs that are characteristic of tipis of the High Plains country between 1860 and 1890.

whole structure. For a foundation, three or four of the poles are tied together and set up first; the additional poles are then arranged between the foundation poles. Some Plains tribes used a four-pole foundation, while others, such as the Cheyenne and Arapaho, used three. The different types of lodges differed from tribe to tribe. Some used lodge poles that extended high above the tops of the lodge, and others used shorter lodge poles.

Traditionally, each tipi had its own place within the camp circle. The camp circle was usually a wide ring with an opening about twenty yards (eighteen meters) long on its east side, with the lodges arranged in a specific order. However, in the winter, lodges were placed at a sheltered site along a river bottom or valley.

Some say the tipi is a reminder of the sacred life circle that has no beginning and no end and that Plains Indians designed their camps as circles within a circle to represent this spiritually held belief.

TIPPECANOE, BATTLE OF

Following the American Revolution, non-Native Americans became seized with the thirst for expanding the borders of the United States. The Ohio River Valley, which lay west of the lands originally settled by British colonists prior to the Revolution, was a logical target for U.S. expansion. Under the leadership of the Shawnee chief Tecumseh and his brother Tenskwatawa, a pan-Indian movement grew in resistance to these plans for U.S. growth. Determined to establish the Ohio River as the line separating the United States from the vast Indian homeland that he envisioned, Tecumseh gathered support for his idea by traveling among tribes from Florida to Wisconsin.

Many Native elders opposed the idea of a confederacy of Indian nations, and most tribes, despite their concern over white encroachments on their lands, believed that it should be up to each individual tribe to decide how to handle its own land.

The defeat of Tenskwatawa (the Shawnee Prophet) at Tippecanoe, Indiana, in 1811. In the absence of his brother, Shawnee leader Tecumseh, Tenskwatawa led an assault on invading U.S. troops that led to the defeat of the Indians and the virtual death of Tecumseh's vision of a pan-Indian alliance.

Nonetheless, Tecumseh's vision was a powerful one, and many followed his lead when he and Tenskwatawa began assembling a band of warriors in 1808 at Tippecanoe, Indiana. In the years that followed, Tecumseh was quite successful in planting the seeds of his pan-Indian alliance, and he even won the grudging praise of William Henry Harrison, then the governor of the territory of Indiana, as a revolutionary leader.

It was on November 7, 1811, however, during Tecumseh's absence from the alliance's headquarters, that Harrison chose to send in soldiers against Tippecanoe, the large Indian village on the banks of the Wabash River. Rather than hold off the troops and buy time until Tecumseh's return, Tenskwatawa, who was known to his followers as the Prophet, ordered a poorly planned assault on the soldiers. As a result of his actions, the Indians were defeated and Tenskwatawa himself was discredited.

The disaster at Tippecanoe spelled the beginning of the end for Tecumseh's promising Indian alliance. Tecumseh kept up his efforts against U.S. encroachments on Indian lands, and he even joined the British in their fight against the United States in the War of 1812. In 1813, however, he was killed in battle on the Thames River. Without his leadership, his great plan for Indian unity went unfulfilled.

SEE ALSO:
Pan-Indian (Intertribal) Movements; Shawnee; Tecumseh.

TIWA PUEBLOS

The Pueblo people of New Mexico are members of three distinct language families—Keresan, Zunian, and Tanoan. The Tanoan language is divided into three dialects—Tiwa, Towa, and Tewa. Four pueblos speak the Tiwa dialect of the Tanoan language; they are Isleta, Picurís, Sandia, and Taos.

A church at the Picurís Pueblo, New Mexico.

A woman harvests fruit off of a saguaro cactus in the U.S. Southwest.

Isleta Pueblo is a southern pueblo located south of Albuquerque, New Mexico. The pueblo has 211,103 acres (85,497 hectares) of land. The 1980 census reported a population of 3,262, and the 1989 Bureau of Indian Affairs (BIA) Labor Force Report listed it at 2,979. The 1990 census reported a population of 2,784. Isleta Pueblo is the largest Tiwa-speaking pueblo and is composed of several communities on the Rio Grande. Isleta Lakes has a campground available to visitors, but no cameras are allowed at the pueblo. For a detailed discussion of the modern tribal government of Isleta Pueblo, see *American Indian Tribal Governments*, by Sharon O'Brien (Norman: University of Oklahoma Press, 1989).

Picurís Pueblo is a northern pueblo located north of Santa Fe. The pueblo has 14,947 acres (6,053 hectares) of land. Population statistics for this pueblo vary. The 1980 census reported a population of 245, and the 1989 BIA Labor Force Report listed it at 221. However, the 1990 census reported a population of 1,867. Picurís is the smallest of the Tiwa-speaking pueblos. The original pueblo, built in the twelfth century, was abandoned after the Pueblo Revolt of 1680 and was reestablished in the early eighteenth century. The Pueblo Cultural Center here has a museum and a restaurant, and camera permits are available at the visitor center.

Sandia Pueblo is a southern pueblo, located south of Santa Fe but north of Albuquerque. The reservation that encompasses Sandia Pueblo has 22,870 acres (9,262 hectares) of land. The 1980 census reported the population at 312, and the 1989 BIA Labor Force Report listed it as 321. However, the 1990 census reported the population at 3,940. Sandia Pueblo itself is a small pueblo within the larger reservation, occupying about 26 acres (10 hectares) near the center of the reservation. Its annual feast day is open to the public, but no cameras are allowed.

Taos Pueblo is a northern pueblo located north

of Santa Fe. The pueblo has 95,341 acres (38,613 hectares) of land. The 1980 census reported a population of 1,951, and the 1989 BIA Labor Force Report listed it at 1,631. The 1990 census reported a population of 4,486. Taos Pueblo is famous for its drums. A national historic site, the pueblo is heavily visited by tourists. An admission fee is charged, and a map marks areas that are off-limits to visitors. Cameras are not allowed on feast days. Taos Pueblo and the nearby town of Taos were famous during the fur-trapping days of the colonial era. Now, the town of Taos is an artist colony with more than ninety art galleries. During the administration of President Richard Nixon, the United States returned to Taos Pueblo ownership of its sacred Blue Lake in the nearby front range of the Rocky Mountains.

Verna Williamson, former governor of Isleta, the largest Tiwa-speaking pueblo.

TOBACCO

Although no one knows the exact origins of tobacco, its existence throughout North, Central, and South America can be traced back at least six thousand years. The tobacco plant is of the genus *Nicotiana*, part of the Solanaceae or nightshade family, which also includes the potato, the pepper, and the deadly, poisonous nightshade. Only two of the sixty known species of tobacco have ever been cultivated: the *Nicotiana rustica* originally grown by Indian cultures in North America, and *Nicotiana tabacum*, which was cultivated primarily in the tropical regions.

Virtually every American Indian culture knew about tobacco, from Canada's eastern woodlands to southern Argentina, from the Atlantic coast to the Pacific. Because it was easy to grow and adaptable to many different soil types, tobacco was even grown by Indians who practiced no other form of

An undated photo of an Indian smoking a pipe. Tobacco has long played a social, commercial, medicinal, and religious role in Native cultures.

agriculture (such as the Haida and Tlingit of the Northwest Pacific Coast region).

Tobacco was important to Native Americans for spiritual, medicinal, and social reasons. For many cultures, such as the Winnebago, it was considered a sacred substance with both supernatural powers and supernatural origins. Tobacco was often offered to the spirits in exchange for their care and good works. These gifts could take the form of cured tobacco thrown on a fire or tobacco leaves left at some sacred spot.

Another example of how tobacco symbolized the contact between the human and spirit worlds was its use by holy people (healers or shamans). When shamans consumed tobacco, it was to feed the spirits inside them. At the same time, ingesting and metabolizing large amounts of nicotine could induce a trancelike state, often resulting in out-of-body experiences. This had the effect of

temporarily transporting holy men into the world of the spirits. Such a trance could also supposedly enable a shaman to divine the future.

Tobacco played an important role in spiritual ceremonies. Ojibwes (Chippewas) believed that the spirits of the supernatural world who inhabited the earth, sky, and water could be soothed and honored by offerings of tobacco and therefore began all their religious and ceremonial occasions with ritual smoking.

In addition to using tobacco for spiritual reasons, healers used tobacco for medicinal purposes. Some ingested it to give themselves the power to diagnose their patients' illnesses, while others blew smoke over the person's body to locate the areas of evil infestation that could then be sucked out with a straw. But healers also often used tobacco directly as a cure. The Winnebagos reduced a patient's pain by rubbing him or her with tobacco spit or by applying wet tobacco leaves or snuff plasters to the afflicted parts of the body. In parts of Mexico, Guatemala, and Peru, it was common to treat tooth- and earaches with tobacco juice or chewing tobac- co, and other cultures, like the Cherokees, used tobacco as both a painkiller and an antiseptic in the treatment of open wounds and snake bites.

Throughout North and South America, tobac- co had hundreds of other medicinal uses, includ- ing the treatment of asthma, rheumatism, chills, fevers, convulsions, intestinal disorders, worms, childbirth pains, headaches, boils, cysts, and even coughs. Tobacco also played an important social role in Native American cultures. Smoking was a well-established after-dinner activity among the Aztecs, for example, long before the Spanish arrived. Although smoking was by far the most widespread method of tobacco consumption, other popular methods included chewing, drinking the juice, tak- ing snuff, and purging with tobacco enemas. By the time Europeans arrived in the Americas, Native people had experimented with every conceivable method of consuming tobacco and had developed the technology necessary for its use.

In many North American cultures, any agree- ment or obligation that was sealed in the presence of tobacco (usually by passing around a pipe) was legally binding. This tradition was often developed into an elaborate and formal ritual, known as the calumet, in which a special pipe was shared among participants, followed by singing and dancing. Pipe sculpting (often out of soapstone or clay) became an art form, and many myths evolved about how humans were given the gift of the pipe, myths that became an important part of their spiritual beliefs. One example is the beautiful Lakota legend of the White Buffalo Calf Woman.

Pipe smoking was less popular in Mexico and Central and South America, where the most pop- ular method of tobacco consumption was the smok- ing of cigars (some of which were up to a foot in length). Tobacco chewing and the drinking of tobacco juice were also quite popular.

Until the first Europeans arrived at the end of the fifteenth century, no one outside the Ameri- can continents had any knowledge of cultivated tobacco. According to some historians, it was not until John Rolfe married Pocahontas, the daugh- ter of a local Powhatan leader, that any European learned about the cultivation of tobacco. Rolfe apparently planted the first crop of tobacco in the Virginia colony of Jamestown, and tobacco became a fortune-founding cash crop when its use caught on in England.

In recent years, it is the sale of tobacco that has become an important issue for Native Americans in the United States. Starting in the 1890s, Indian nations were allowed to operate smoke shops that sold tobacco products to reservation residents at a reduced price. This was possible because, although Indian nations had to pay federal tax on tobacco products, they were exempt from paying a state tax.

Problems arose in recent years when some states realized they were losing tax money because non- Indians were going to the reservations to purchase their tobacco products and were therefore not pay- ing the state sales tax. State tax commissioners began raiding reservation smoke shops and confis- cating all of their tobacco products. In some states, officers confiscated tobacco products from non- Indian customers as they left the reservations.

State taxation rights versus the rights of Indian nations rapidly became an explosive issue in the United States court system. In 1993, the Supreme Court ruled that the state of New York could limit the amount of untaxed tobacco products sold to reservation shops strictly to the needs of the reser- vations' residents. Some tribal nations, including several in Oklahoma, have signed compacts with the state in which their territory resides, agreeing to pay a fee in lieu of taxes for products sold to non- Indians at tribal smoke shops. Others, however, consider paying a state tax and a tribal tax as dou- ble taxation and have refused to sign such a com- pact. In these cases, litigation is still pending in the courts.

— P. Press

SEE ALSO:
Calumet Pipe and Dance; Pocahontas.

SUGGESTED READINGS:

Goodman, Jordan. *Tobacco in History: The Cultures of Dependence.* New York: Routledge, 1993.

Hurt, R. D. *Indian Agriculture in America.* Lawrence: University Press of Kansas, 1987.

Paper, J. *Offering Smoke: The Sacred Pipe and Native American Religion.* Moscow: The University of Idaho Press, 1988.

TOHONO O'ODHAM

The Tohono O'odham, the desert people formerly known as the Papago, reside in the Sonoran Desert region in what is currently southern Arizona and northern Mexico. Many of the people are trilingual, reflecting their history: They speak O'odham, Spanish, and English. Thought to be descended from the Hohokam, the Tohono O'odham people first encountered the Spaniards in the 1600s. Also known as the "Two Villagers," the O'odham divided their time between a summer village where they irrigated with floodwaters and a winter home higher in the mountains where permanent water was available. Although they practiced some agriculture, the O'odham people hunted and gathered, and they adapted their technology cleverly to the desert environment. They also traded with other tribes for what was unavailable in the desert.

Spanish colonization began with the Jesuit Father Eusabio Kino's exploration and establishment of missions in the Sonoran Desert. A silver strike in 1736 heralded an onslaught of Spanish fortune seekers into the area. By 1751, one O'odham band began to attack missions and ranches in an attempt to drive the Spaniards south again. Spain retreated but reestablished its presence in the O'odham country by 1754. By that time, the Apaches, pushed westward by settlers, began to raid the O'odham people, who then allied themselves with the Spanish against the Apaches. The O'odham became devout Catholics, but it was their own brand of Catholicism, created to fill their needs.

In 1821, Mexico won its independence from Spain, and the Tohono O'odham people experienced an increased northern migration of Mexicans who took over their lands. The O'odham defended their territory in armed conflict from May 1840 to June 1843, when they yielded to Mexico. In 1853, the United States completed the Gadsden Purchase from Mexico, which resulted in half the O'odham people being in Mexico

A Tohono O'odham village in Arizona.

and half in the United States. They continued to lose land in Sonora, Mexico, until a proclamation was signed in 1928 by President Elias Calles establishing a community land grant of approximately 7,675 acres (3,108 hectares). The O'odham were able to largely ignore what was for them the artificial U.S.–Mexican border until recently, when tighter controls made it difficult for them to move easily throughout their territory.

Tohono O'odham people in the United States had their first reservation, the San Xavier Reservation, established in 1874. During the early twentieth century, both the establishment of day schools to replace boarding schools by the government and the church and the introduction of the cattle business among the O'odham people greatly influenced the development of their lifestyle. Nevertheless, running cattle in the sparse desert environment was often inadequate economically, and many O'odham people became wage laborers. They provided most of the labor force for picking cotton in Arizona until the operation became mechanized.

In the 1980s, approximately half of the seventeen thousand Tohono O'odham people lived on their three reservations in Arizona: San Xavier (71,095 acres/28,793 hectares), Gila Bend (10,337 acres/4,186 hectares) and Tohono O'odham (2,774,370 acres/1,123,620 hectares) at Sells. The tribal authority receives income from mining leas-

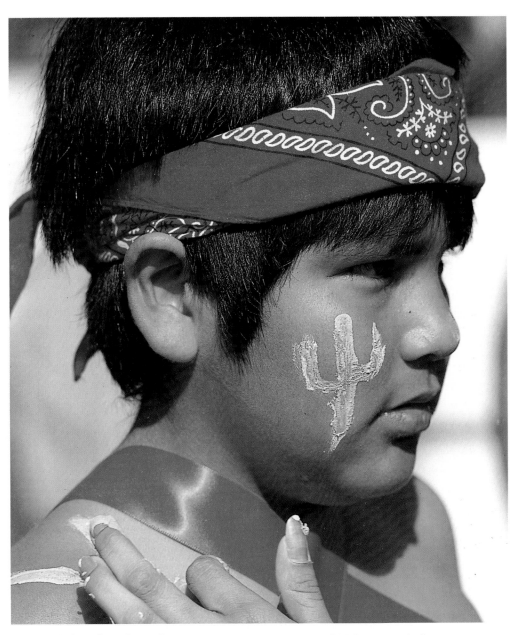

A member of the Tohono O'odham youth dance group prepares for a performance in Casa Grande, Arizona.

es and the lease funds from the Kitt Peak National Observatory, which is on O'odham land. The Tohono O'odham people have also recently established a gambling casino on the San Xavier Reservation. While per capita income is low and many of the people find it necessary to move to outlying cities to find employment, the O'odham maintain a singularly strong identity and lifestyle. Their lifestyle is expressed in what they call their "Himdag," or way of life. This includes concepts of culture, history, values, beliefs, customs, and language.

Perhaps because they have long lived on remote, unfriendly desert lands, the Tohono O'odham people have been able to maintain some of their ancestral lands and develop their own lifestyle, albeit one that has adapted to the dominant culture in North America. Today, they are actively teaching their native language and also converting it into a written language for the first time, so that it can continue to be used as a live language. The O'odham people have established an educational system that teaches their young the things they need to know to survive on the outside but that also incorporate their own teachings. In 1994, a tribal history that they commissioned was published for use in their schools.

SEE ALSO:
Apache; Arizona; Catholic Church in the Spanish Empire; Hohokam; Mexico, Indigenous People of; New Spain; Pima; Spain.

TOLTEC

North of the Valley of Mexico, in the southern reaches of present-day Hidalgo, the Toltecs emerged as the premier Mesoamerican people during the centuries before the Aztecas (Mexicas) moved into the Valley of Mexico around the twelfth century. The urban area and ceremonial center called Tula, the Toltecs' capital, was situated in a highland river valley that supplied the city with water. It is very probable that the migrations into Tula, which reached a peak population of about forty thousand between the tenth and twelfth centuries, may have come from many different directions. Unlike the Aztecs, the Toltecs did not rule a far-flung empire. Most of their activities, except trade, were carried out in or near Tula.

One class of priests, craftspeople, and merchants (called the Nonoalca) seemed to have played a pivotal role in making the Toltecs the most influential group of people in Mesoamerica between roughly

A yoke carved out of stone, believed to be of Toltec or Aztec origin.

A mask, found in Mexico, of Toltec or Aztec origin.

900 and 1200 C.E. Various sources indicate that the Nonoalca were of various ethnic backgrounds and that they spoke several languages (including Nahuatl, the language later used by the Aztecs and the Nahua today in central Mexico).

At its height, Tula covered 5.4 square miles (14 square kilometers), including nearly half a square mile (1.3 square kilometers) of uninhabited swamp ("El Salitre"). This area, which was used mainly as a source of materials for baskets, may have given Tula its original Toltec name, Tollan, which meant "place of the reeds."

Private homes at Tula have been nearly always found in groups of three to five, each containing several rooms, all facing onto a common interior courtyard. This pattern indicates the presence of extended families who lived together and acted as an economic as well as a family unit. Each group of houses was often fenced off from other clusters, showing an interest in privacy. Entrances often were built into halls that turned 90 degrees to ensure the privacy of occupants. The houses were well adapted to their highland environment, with thick adobe walls that retained cool air during hot summer afternoons. The same structures also held warmth during frosty winter mornings. Drainage pipes were constructed to siphon occasional heavy rains that fell on Tula, and stone foundations helped prevent moisture from seeping into homes through the floors.

Like most other Mesoamerican peoples, the Toltecs surrounded their major city with a roughly circular network of agricultural villages. Agriculture around Tula was made possible by extensive irrigation from the nearby river. The area is laced with ditches and canals, a sign that water was moved from place to place in large quantities. Some farm fields also were terraced, and many private home-clusters also contained intensively cultivated domestic gardens where people raised condiments, herbs, and medicinal plants.

Toltec traders covered an area that included the entire Yucatán Peninsula and most of the northern reaches of Maya highland country. In the north, traders sought precious materials, such as turquoise, copper, gold, and silver on the arid steppes of what is now northern Mexico. Tula was a manufacturing center for such objects as obsidian cutting tools and other crafts.

By about 1170 C.E., the Toltecs succumbed to invaders from the north whom they called Chichimecs ("Dog People"). Lean, hungry, and barbarous, they arrived behind a barrage of bows and arrows and stayed to absorb the culture of the Valley of Mexico.

SEE ALSO:
Aztec; Chichimec; Maya; Mexico, Indigenous People of; Olmec.

TOMAHAWK CHOP

The Tomahawk Chop, a hand motion made while an athletic team with an Indian name competes, was created for the Florida State University Seminoles. To perform a "chop," fans bend their arms at the elbows, hold their hands straight out with palm turned inward, and then lift their arms in the air, bringing them straight down in a chopping motion.

From Florida State, the Tomahawk Chop spread to other sports teams that use Indians as a mascot or symbol. Most people identify the motion with the Atlanta Braves, thanks to the exposure given the team through its nationally broadcast games on cable and its recent appearances in the World Series. At Braves' games, fans combine the chopping motion with a variety of other actions that have, through stereotyped portrayals in television and the movies, become associated with American Indians. These actions include the steady and somewhat ominous drumbeat ("BOOM-boom-boom-boom. BOOM-boom-boom-boom") that people often associate with the appearance of "Indians" and a "chant" that is only a bit removed from the grunts and "ughs" that characterized Native "talking" in old movies.

These actions by sports fans are considered insulting by most Indian people because they betray a lack of understanding of Indians as real people. Instead, such actions seize images that are stereotypical and portray them as cute, funny, or grotesque. To American Indians, this type of subtle racism is painful in view of Native people's history once Europeans arrived on the North American continent. This history includes the wholesale removal of

Outside the Metrodome in Minneapolis during the 1991 Minnesota–Atlanta World Series, a group of American Indians and their supporters protest the use of chants and tomahawks by fans of the Atlanta Braves. Saying that such practices are racist and make a mockery of Native traditions and beliefs, some of the demonstrators make their point with signs that draw comparisons with racist portrayals of Blacks and Jews.

Native people from their homelands to reservations and concentration camps, termination programs shrinking the Indian land base, funding cuts, the suppression of Native religions, the desecration of sacred sites and burial grounds, and the teaching of a false history based on centuries of misconceptions and misrepresentations of the cultures and of the effect of Europeans on those cultures.

The chop, the drumbeats, the "chanting," the mascots, the emblems, and virtually all the other images that are integrated into the chop portray Indian people as savage, hostile, or uncivilized. Critics—both Native and non-Native alike—have pointed out that these images mock a race of people and their religions, languages, value systems, and lives. Although it is considered to be done in fun, the same mockery of other racial, religious, and ethnic groups would not be tolerated.

In recent years, some progress has been made in bringing to light these offenses to Indian people's spirituality, dignity, and identity. Many public school systems have debated the wisdom of retaining team names, mascots, and symbols that draw upon Indian themes, and some schools—fewer—have actually changed their nicknames. For example, Marquette University's sports teams, for decades called the Warriors, are now the Golden Eagles. Some newspapers—again, a very few—have stopped referring to team nicknames that mock Indian cultures. (The prime target of this action has been the Washington Redskins, a team whose nickname is termed "offensive slang" and "a disparaging term for a Native American" in many dictionaries. Knowing full well that the Cleveland Indians baseball team will probably never change their nickname, some observers wonder when they will alter their logo, which is a grotesque caricature of a grinning, war-whooping, red-faced Indian.)

During the World Series between the Atlanta Braves and the Minnesota Twins, protesters organized picket lines outside the stadiums of both teams directed at baseball's tolerance for the mocking of Native rituals. During these protests, it was pointed out that Minnesotans might be especially concerned about such offenses considering the fact that American Indians are a "minority" of significant proportions in the state of Minnesota.

Although the protests and commentaries, many of them appearing in non-Native sports publica-

tions, did not put an end to the Tomahawk Chop, they did produce some interesting side effects. For example, television viewers could not help but notice that some of the Braves' better-known fans, such as team owner Ted Turner and his wife, Jane Fonda, and former Georgia governor and U.S. president Jimmy Carter, were caught on camera performing a modified version of the chop. Instead of holding their hands at a right angle to the ground and moving them up and down in a chopping motion, they held them out in front of them parallel to the ground and moved them back and forth. Some observers noted that although the gesture was definitely an improvement over the original version of the chop, it was still done in time to the drumbeat and the chant of the crowd—and that it now resembled another stereotyped image, that of an old chief drawing his hand out in front of him to signify "peace," "a long, long distance," or "many moons ago."

— S. S. Davis / M. J. Sachner

SEE ALSO:

Baseball; European Attitudes Toward Indigenous Peoples; Hollywood, Indians and Indian Images in; Sacred Sites; Scalping; Sockalexis, Louis.

TONTO AND THE LONE RANGER

SEE Silverheels, Jay.

TOURISM

Next to gaming, tourism provides the most money for many Indian nations. In the last two decades of the twentieth century, non-Indians became increasingly fascinated with items and activities that are considered part of Native cultures. More and more tourists—not just North Americans but people from around the globe—attend powwows and other events where Indians gather; and once they attend, they buy things relating to or made by American Indians. Many of these items, such as dream catchers and medicine wheels, have become so popular that children make them in

A huge passenger ship makes its way through a bay in Juneau, Alaska. Native groups are beginning to profit from the interest among non-Indians all over the world in Native American cultures. Many American Indian groups are attracting tourists to their own communities; others benefit by their proximity to other attractions.

school and adults hang them from the rearview mirrors in their cars.

In response to this fascination with all things Indian, many tribal governments have begun catering to tourists, presenting contest powwows and other "noncultural" Indian events. These events allow non-Indians to watch dancers, study colorful regalia—even join in the dancing—without violating the privacy or sacred nature of spiritual events that are not open to the public. Some tribes have set up replicas of pre-Columbian villages to attract tourists, and others stage dramatic interpretations of their history in the form of plays. Indian-owned and -operated museums are gaining in business as non-Indians look for crafts and other artifacts from past and present Native cultures.

Indian people and their communities are by no means the only ones to have earned a living manufacturing or selling items that have Indian themes. In fact, most of the goods sold in North America, particularly in the United States, that have an "Indian" look to them have typically been made by non-Natives. Because so many non-Indians were

selling art and craftwork as "authentic American Indian" work, Congress passed the Native American Arts and Crafts Act in 1990. This act was meant to protect buyers from purchasing products that were not Indian-made, but now beadwork, basketry, and other items are sold as "Indian-style" or "Indian-type." Because so many of the items can be mass-produced, non-Indian retailers can sell them cheaper than truly Indian-made items.

Realizing the profits to be made "selling" Indians to people from non-Native cultures, many states and communities have moved into the tourism market, marketing their homegrown Native cultures as a product. For example, one of Oklahoma's tourism department slogans is "Oklahoma, Native America." The state even sponsors the biggest event in Oklahoma that purports to be Indian—Red Earth Days. Although Red Earth Days does attract many Indian people as participants and spectators, some observers feel that this event bears a striking resemblance to Wild West shows, which also feature Indians, and that it serves the same purpose: to bring tourists into the state. In many places, such as South Dakota, for example, non-Indians own and operate "Indian villages" and other "Indian" attractions that do little to teach non-Indians about actual Native cultures. And in a state like South Dakota, where Indians living on Pine Ridge and other reservations experience rates of unemployment, poverty, and mortality that are among the highest of—and in many cases higher than—any in the United States, these attractions do virtually nothing to improve the economic lot of Indian people in the state. In fact, even on reservations where Indians have catered to tourists by giving them what they want—a chance to be dazzled by the scenery, relax, have fun, and take pictures of Indian dancing—these forms of entertainment do not always translate into profits for Native communities. Non-Indian-owned businesses nearby, such as restaurants and motels, often make much of the profit.

Some tribes have turned the tables, however. The Eastern Band of Cherokees in North Carolina have managed to draw tourists to their reservation with trendy Indian stores and events and even a tribally operated motel. The area thrives with tourists who want to see Indians, complete with beads and feathers, and the tribe caters to that. Tourism has thus added greatly to the tribe's economic stability. And yet, as some members of the tribe and other Native people have pointed out, this kind of economic growth may have a price tag attached—the loss of tribal identity and authenticity, not just in the eyes of the tourists who come to see the sights, but in the lives and character of the tribe itself.

SEE ALSO:
Buffalo Bill's Wild West Show; Gaming; New Age Movement; Powwows; Red Earth Festival; Regalia.

TOWA PUEBLOS

The Pueblo people of New Mexico are members of three distinct language families—Keresan, Zunian, and Tanoan. The Tanoan language is divided into

Laura Fragua, an artist at Jemez, New Mexico, the last Towa-speaking pueblo.

Maxine Toya at work on a group of unpainted, unfired figurines at her studio in Jemez, New Mexico.

three dialects—Tiwa, Towa, and Tewa. With the abandonment of Pecos Pueblo, Jemez is the last remaining Towa-speaking pueblo.

Jemez is a southern pueblo, located north of Albuquerque. The pueblo has 89,623 acres (35,849 hectares) of land. The 1980 census reported a population of 2,181, and the 1989 Bureau of Indian Affairs Labor Force Report listed it at 2,378. The 1990 census reported a population of only 1,615. Jemez is located in an area of wilderness and natural beauty. As the last remaining Towa-speaking pueblo, it absorbed the Towa-speaking survivors of Pecos Pueblo when Pecos was abandoned in the 1830s. Cameras are not permitted at the pueblo, which is known for its baskets made of yucca fronds.

Pecos Pueblo was a thriving commercial center when the Spanish arrived in the Southwest in the sixteenth century. Before the historic southward migration of the Comanche Nations onto the southern Great Plains in the eighteenth century, Pecos Pueblo was the center of contact for the Pueblos of the Rio Grande Valley and the Plains Apaches. Annual trade fairs at Pecos Pueblo were spectacu-lar events; entire bands of Plains Apaches camped for weeks outside the pueblo, trading the by-products of the buffalo Plains for the agricultural produce and pottery of the Pueblos. After the Plains Apaches were displaced from the Plains by the Comanches, Pecos continued as a point of contact with the Comanches, but its population declined until finally it was abandoned in the 1830s.

SEE ALSO:

Apache; Comanche; Keresan Pueblos; New Mexico; Tewa Pueblos; Tiwa Pueblos; Zuni.

TOXIC WASTE DUMPS, ARCTIC

The pollution of Native lands in the northern areas of North America has become pervasive, from the St. Regis, or Akwesasne, Reserve (which straddles the U.S.–Canadian border in New York, Quebec, and Ontario) into the Arctic and nearby lands, such as James Bay. During the late twentieth cen-

Aipilik Innuksuk of the Inuit fishes through a hole in the ice on a trip to Uguqjualik, Northwest Territories, Canada. The Arctic has become perhaps the final region in North America to feel the effects of environmental pollution.

tury, Native lands in the Arctic have become the last frontier in North America for environmental contamination.

As if to illustrate just how pervasive pollution of the entire earth has become, studies of Inuit (Eskimo) women's breast milk in the late twentieth century revealed abnormally high levels of PCBs. Toxic levels of this carcinogenic chemical have spread from emissions sources in the lower latitudes of North America into the oceanic food chain of the Arctic. More PCBs were dumped into the Arctic environment by military installations. Many Inuit people have been poisoned by eating contaminated fish and marine mammals, their major source of protein for thousands of years.

Studies around the rim of Hudson Bay, conducted by Dr. Eric Dewailly of Laval University in 1988, found that nursing mothers' milk contained more than twice the level of PCBs (3.5 parts per million) considered "safe" by the Canadian government. The fish that most Inuit eat act as concentrators of PCBs and other toxic materials in the food chain. By eating the fish, people take part in the same diffusion of the chemicals.

Scientists have found more than PCBs in Inuit mothers' milk. According to author Winona La Duke, "Related contaminants include radioactive cesium, DDT, toxaphene, and other pesticides," most of which have been banned in North America but are still used in many other countries.

The Togiak Salmon Cannery in Alaska. Both the fishing industry and Native people who depend on fish for food have felt the effects of higher levels of toxins in contaminated fish.

Toxins are collecting in peoples' bodies because the Arctic itself is becoming a dump for the atmosphere worldwide. Dr. Lyle Lockhart, an employee of the Canadian government's Fisheries and Oceans Department in Winnipeg, Manitoba, says that toxic materials emitted in the warmer regions of the atmosphere sometimes circulate in the air for years, collecting, and descending in the air over the Arctic and Antarctic. Lockhart cited toxaphene used in cotton fields thousands of miles (kilometers) from the Mackenzie River has been found in Canada's Northwest Territories. (Toxaphene is a generic name for chlorinated camphene, which is used as an insecticide. It is dangerous to dairy animals, and in high exposure, it enters fatty tissue in the nerve sheath surrounding people's nerves and is thus extremely hazardous to our nervous systems.) The Canadian government has caught fish in the Mackenzie with toxaphene in their livers. Larger animals, including human beings, concentrate the toxins in their bodies, thereby storing the substance over a prolonged period of time. Worst hit may be the polar bear, which eats almost nothing but fish. One study indicates that the polar bear may become extinct by the year 2006 because of sterility caused by PCBs.

On the far northwest coast of Alaska, Inuit people have been fighting the U.S. Atomic Energy Commission (AEC) since the late 1950s, when the agency proposed to demonstrate the peaceful uses of atomic energy by blowing open a new harbor at Point Hope with an atomic blast. The government shelved the plan, called Operation Chariot, in 1962. But then, without telling the Inuits, the federal government turned parts of their homeland into a nuclear dump. The dump contained debris gathered from within one mile (1.6 kilometers) of ground zero at a Nevada atomic test site. The purpose of the experiment was to test the toxicity of radiation in an Arctic environment. The dump experiment was carried out by the U.S. Geological Survey under license from the AEC. The fact that the area was occupied by Native people seemed not to matter to the government.

The Inuit did not learn of the nuclear dump until Dan O'Neill, a researcher at the University of Alaska, made public documents he had found as he researched a book on the abandoned plan to blow a nuclear harbor in the coast. For many years, the Inuit in the area have suffered a cancer rate "that far exceeds the national average." The government acknowledges that soil in the area contains "trace amounts" of radiation but denies that its experiment is causing the Inuits' increased cancer rate. According to O'Neill, the nuclear dump was clearly illegal and contained "a thousand times . . . the allowable standard for this kind of nuclear burial."

Point Hope, the closest settlement to the dump, is an Inuit village of seven hundred people, most of whom make a living as whalers. It is one of the oldest continuously occupied town sites in North America. Mayor David Stone, a leader in the fight against the dump, said, "We feel betrayed." Jeslie Kaleak, mayor of North Slope Borough, which includes Point Hope and seven other settlements, added, "I can't tell you how angry I am that they considered our home to be nothing but a big wasteland. . . . They didn't give a damn about people who live up here."

The environmental devastation of remote areas in the Arctic is wrenching, but one must realize that whole societies of Native people are crumbling along with the environment on which they depend. In 1960, before widespread energy development on Alaska's North Slope, the suicide rate among Native people there was 13 per 100,000, comparable to averages in the United States as a whole.

By 1970, the rate had risen to 25 per 100,000; by 1986, the rate had risen to 67.6 per 100,000. Homicide rates by the middle 1980s were three times the average in the United States as a whole, between 22.9 and 26.6 per 100,000 people, depending on which study is used. Death rates from homicide and suicide appear linked to rising alcoholism. In the mid-1980s, 79 percent of Native suicide victims had some alcohol in their blood at the time of death. Slightly more than half (54 percent) were legally intoxicated.

It is not clear whether the deteriorating Arctic environment may be linked directly with the overall decline in the quality of life among Native peoples. Few will dispute the point, however, that the plight of Native cultures in North America has long gone hand in hand with the destruction and degradation of their homelands.

SEE ALSO:

Akwesasne (St. Regis Reservation), Pollution of; Inuit; James Bay Hydro-Electric Project.

SUGGESTED READING:

Grinde, Donald A., Jr., and Bruce E. Johansen. *Ecocide of Native America: Environmental Destruction of Indian Lands and Peoples.* Santa Fe, NM: Clear Light, 1994.

TOYS AND GAMES

In virtually every culture and society imaginable, toys and games are constants in children's lives. The forms and styles of play may vary from society to society, and even within many societies, depending on factors such as age, geography, racial or ethnic background, family income, and personal choice, but few would argue that children like to play. Many cultures engage in traditional forms of play for specific reasons. For example, children may play certain games at certain times of the year and for specific ceremonial or traditional reasons. In most Christian cultures—and even in some non-Christian cultures that celebrate the coming of spring—children hunt for candy and eggs on Easter Sunday. Jewish children spin a small top called a dreidel at Hanukkah time or search for hidden prizes as part of the ritual at the Seder, or Passover dinner. Although most American Indian youngsters play the same kinds of games and with the same kinds of toys as most North American kids, there are many games and toys that are part of their tribal background, and some of these are popular within many Native communities today.

Like children from other "minority" cultures in North America, many Native children play games that are similar to those played by their great-grandparents as children. They sometimes even use contemporary versions of toys that their elders played with. For example, a game called snow-snake was and is still played during the winter by many Eastern Woodland Indians. The object was to see how far the snake, a long thin wooden rod, could be thrown along a trough dug in the snow. The game was played by the men and boys of the tribe, sometimes with the elders betting on their favorite snakes. Other games of dexterity included archery, lacrosse, cup and pin, ball games, and races.

In traditional Native cultures, as in most non-Native cultures, girls enjoyed playing with dolls. They also played house, asking their parents to help

A set of Plains Indian dolls from the late 1800s, made out of hide, beads, and hair. Like children in most societies, Native dolls have traditionally featured clothing and other characteristics that remind them of their own culture.

A traditional Klamath game from Oregon.

them make dwellings, such as hogans, tipis, or wig-wams, that usually resembled those of their parents. Other kinds of play resembled familiar patterns of today. Often the younger girls would gather up all their dolls and houses to play by themselves. When the boys found them setting up a little Indian camp complete with dolls, food, and lodges, they would plan an attack. This is one of the ways that Indian children's toys and games reflected the world in which they lived, especially following contact with European colonizers. Through this kind of play they learned the serious business of surviving. But they also had amusements that were just for fun, such as cat's cradle, spinning tops, and stick games, that they could play quietly within the lodge when the weath-er was bad or an illness kept them inside.

European contact introduced Native children to a host of other types of games and toys, all of which they adapted to suit their own ideas of hav-ing fun. Cards, checkers, and button games became popular among many Native people, including chil-dren. Native children made cards from pieces of tanned deer or moose hide, cutting them in the familiar rectangular shapes and painting pictures or shapes on the front. While buttons were often obtained from non-Indian traders, they could make checkers out of slices of deer horn or peach pits. Sometimes a family might have European toys as a result of trading, but usually they made their own versions from the materials on hand.

Today, particularly at powwows and ceremoni-als, young Native Americans still play many of the old games. Indian football is a very popular sport among both males and females. The football is about as big as a softball, but it is made from deer hide stuffed with deer or buffalo hair. There are very few rules; the primary one is that females can kick, carry, steal, or lie on the ball—for girls and women, the game is no-holds-barred! Males are only allowed to carry the ball when it is free. The game is played until one side tallies the winning score of twelve field goals. Score is kept by an elder, who uses sticks to keep count of the goals, and often a large audience cheers their favorites to victory.

Because virtually all Indian children play the same games and use the same toys as other North American children, they help support an economy that is constantly trying to figure out new ways to convince consumers to keep buying. Playing with traditional toys that have not changed very much—dolls and houses that resemble the people and places where they now live, for example—or playing games that their elders played a long time ago, such as football, give Indian children the chance to adapt old ways of having fun to modern times while retaining many of the traditional ties that help keep Native cultures alive.

— K. Wood

SEE ALSO:
Children.

TRADE AND INTERCOURSE ACT

SEE Indian Trade and Intercourse Act.

TRAIL OF BROKEN TREATIES

The 1972 Trail of Broken Treaties was a nationwide demonstration of concern over issues involving Indian people and the U.S. government. It grew out of an idea developed by members of the American Indian Movement (AIM), who sought to figure out a way of both dramatizing their concerns and delivering them to the government in Washington, D.C.

AIM members decided that one way of gaining media coverage for their efforts would be to form caravans of hundreds of Indians from all over the United States and drive into Washington, D.C., on a specific day. It was agreed that the day would be November 3, just before the 1972 U.S. presidential election, and that the groups would meet at the Bureau of Indian Affairs (BIA) building.

The two directors of the trail's executive council were Russell Means, a long-time AIM member and one of its chief spokespersons, and AIM

cofounder Dennis Banks. Means was selected to organize the first caravan, which was to start in Seattle, Washington, and Banks was chosen to rally the second caravan from San Francisco, California. Recruits, endorsements, and financial support were gathered for the Trail of Broken Treaties.

The first two caravans headed east, stopping along the way at reservations and Indian communities within reasonable driving distance. The BIA had been instructed not to assist any of the different groups that were heading east, and according to some, it did its best to discourage the event and to slow the caravans. Yet when the caravans reached the different reservations, people greeted them enthusiastically, anxious to add their issues and problems to the growing list to be presented at the BIA building in Washington.

The caravan stopped in St. Paul, Minnesota, to organize and write out the grievances to be presented. Participants came up with a document called the Twenty Points, which summarized the participants' views of problems confronting Native people and the federal government and provided a program of reform that the Indians would support. It also presented a framework for considering the status of Indian tribes and the nature of their relationship with the U.S. government.

When the combined caravan arrived in Washington on November 3, they began a series of meetings and confrontations with officials—and with the complex Washington bureaucracy—that would prove both frustrating and enlightening. The trail's organizers had asked to hold religious services at three Arlington Cemetery sites where prominent Indian soldiers were buried. They learned upon arriving in Washington, however, that the request had been denied because the services were too closely related to the group's political activities.

Despite this setback, the group had been told that they would receive more than talk when they arrived in Washington, so hundreds of the activists went to the BIA to see if arrangements could be made for their stay in Washington. As the trail's steering committee talked with BIA officials, others from the caravan lounged around the BIA building's ground floor waiting for the results. By late afternoon, BIA security guards tried to clear the building of the group, who refused to leave without their steering committee. This is when the

Refusing to leave the Bureau of Indian Affairs headquarters in Washington, D.C., without a fair hearing of their grievances, hundreds of Trail of Broken Treaties participants blocked the BIA entrance on November 3, 1972.

peaceful demonstration started to become contentious and even violent.

When the Indians refused to leave the building, the BIA security began using their clubs on the group. The security guards were quickly overpowered and thrown out of the building by the Indians, who then barricaded the building against the police. As BIA employees escaped through windows, police surrounded the building in an effort to keep other Indians from getting in.

The group occupying the BIA building finally numbered about four hundred. With more media coverage than they had planned—and even some unexpected support from people in the public at large—the group decided to occupy the building until the government agreed to negotiate their Twenty Points.

Finally, after receiving far more coverage of their concerns than they had expected, the occupiers agreed to leave the building after being promised that no criminal charges would be filed and that caravan participants would receive about $70,000 for travel expenses. Although the Twenty Points eventually dropped by the wayside, the U.S. government had, however, taken notice of the existence of the American Indian Movement, and in the years to come, its relation with AIM would become increasingly confrontational.

The aftermath of the Trail of Broken Treaties and the BIA occupation included the news that some of the demonstrators had found papers documenting activities of the government directed toward—and often against—Indian people in the twentieth century. After photocopying the documents, AIM returned them to the BIA.

Many consider the Trail of Broken Treaties, along with the BIA occupation and subsequent confrontations at Wounded Knee (in South Dakota), and Alcatraz Island (off the coast of California) to have marked the beginning of a very tumultuous decade for Indian people.

— S. S. Davis

See also:

Alcatraz Island, Occupation of; American Indian Movement; Banks, Dennis; Bureau of Indian Affairs; Crow Dog, Leonard; Means, Russell; Self-determination; Wounded Knee, Confrontation at (1973).